"Every parent who is planning to send their child to college over the next few years absolutely needs to read this book. This is going to make the biggest difference of sending their child to their dream school or having to fall back to their safety school."
  – Manuel Fabriquer, CCPS
    President and CEO of www.CollegePlanningABC.com

"An easy, understandable flow for the reader to follow...shows the family a real life situation. The reader will realize that attending a more expensive college or private college may indeed be less costly than a public institution."
  – Jeff Foley, CPA
    President of Carolina Tax Advisory Group

"The college admissions process has become increasingly complex and confusing. Ryan helps families understand the private schools can be affordable options and should not be ruled out."
  – Mary Jan Freeman, M.A.Ed.
    President of The Davidson Center
    Certified Educational Planner, Member of IECA

"This book provides a practical and easily understood approach to better understanding the college access process for students, parents, and other professionals. I am glad to have a book/referral source for the thousands of students and families we work with!"
  – Renée Anthony Leak
    Director of High Schools and ThinkCOLLEGE

COLLEGE AID
for Middle Class America

Solutions to Paying WHOLESALE vs. RETAIL

C. Ryan Clark

TUITION PUBLISHING

Charlotte, NC

COLLEGE AID for Middle Class America:
Solutions to Paying WHOLESALE vs. RETAIL
C. Ryan Clark

Copyright © 2011 by C. Ryan Clark

Published by:
Tuition Publishing
10130 Mallard Creek Road
Suite 300
Charlotte, NC 28269

ISBN: 978-0-9831941-1-8

Library of Congress Control Number: 2010942015

First Edition, 2011

Published in the United States of America

For more information, visit www.CollegeAidForMiddleClass.com

This book is dedicated to my family: Rosie, Caden, and Carlene. The book is also dedicated to my mother and the memory of my loving father.

Never be afraid to fail and learn from your mistakes. Life is not about how many times you succeed or get knocked down, but how many times you get back up after you stumble.

"*The mind that opens to a new idea never comes back to its original size.*"
– Albert Einstein

Table of Contents

Foreword

High School . . . Friends . . . GPA . . . Athletics . . . SAT . . .
Service Hours . . . Finances . . . College?

Where does the time go when one enters the high school scene? You enter as a freshman one day, and a few years later, you are trying to figure out what to do with your life after high school. The challenges and obstacles facing students today when applying to college can be very overwhelming and stressful for both the student and family members. These challenges only escalate when more than one child is involved. Where in the world does one begin?

When your child is in high school wanting to attend college, there are so many avenues to cover and questions to ask. *Which college should I attend? What do colleges look for in an applicant? What is the difference between private colleges and state colleges? What is involved in the application process? How do I know whether or not a particular college is the "right fit" for me? How much can my family contribute? Will my parents have to go into debt or use their retirement funds? How much can I borrow? What loan options are available? Are there any tax advantages? What has to be included on the financial aid forms? . . .* The list goes on.

Wouldn't it be wonderful not to have to worry about any of these questions? Would it not be ideal to have someone who looks out for your best interest, considering that the price of a college for just one student now ranges from **$60,000** at a state college to over **$200,000** for many private colleges and that the cost continues to rise 8% to 15% a year?

At last, at last. At last, there is a uniquely skilled individual who is also a parent, a small business owner, a college advisor, and someone who has helped and guided hundreds of families reduce the cost of college. Ryan Clark offers a guide and shares his insight into the "college game." This book lays out in detail easy-to-follow, step-by-step strategies, common mistakes most parents make that cost them money, and the inside secrets of the college admissions and financial aid processes. He provides parents with the tools necessary to answer the college cost catastrophe.

Ryan's advice will help many families with the financial elephant of paying for college while protecting their current lifestyle and future retirement plans. His true-to-life solutions and easy-to-understand steps are a must-read for any family that has children planning on attending college. So what are you waiting for? Turn the page, master the game plan, and let the games begin, because the clock is ticking. . .

    – Bonnie Wright

      Parent of a son who is a junior in college

Warning – Disclaimer

This book is written to provide information and general guidance. The author and the publisher is not, and did not intend to be, engaging in rendering legal, accounting, or other professional services. Please refer to varying state and/or local laws, rules and/or regulations, and please engage in the services of a competent legal and/or accounting professional if assistance is needed or required.

It is not the purpose of this book to reprint all the information that is otherwise available to authors and/or publishers but instead to complement, amplify, and supplement other texts. Neither the author nor the publisher assumes any responsibility for errors, omissions, or contradictory interpretation of the subject matter. You are urged to read all the available material about college planning and college financial aid and to tailor the information to your individual needs.

Although the information in the book has been proven effective, the reader or said purchaser assumes all responsibility for any and all usage. This text should be considered as a general guide, and every effort has been made to make this book as complete and as accurate as possible. However, there may be mistakes, both typographical and in content. You, said purchaser, reader, or user of this material, solely assume all responsibility for any and all such usage. Directly or indirectly, the author and the publisher shall have neither liability nor responsibility to any person or entity with respect to any loss or damage caused by the information contained in this book. Moreover, the book contains information that is current only up to the printing date.

With this in mind, the author believes confidently that the information in this book may be used safely, legally, and successfully to educate and entertain readers on the simple steps to obtain *Affordable Solutions for the High Cost of Education*™. **If you do not wish to be bound by the above, you may return this book to the publisher for a full refund.**

College Aid for Middle Class System
Steps to Success

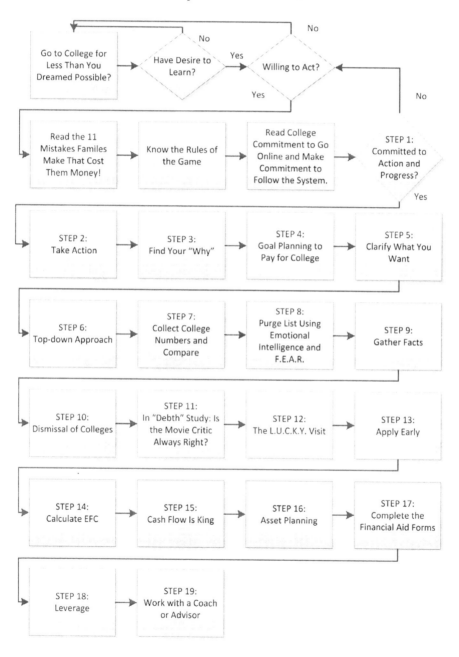

CHAPTER 1

Here Come the Tears

As I looked up from my desk, I briefly made eye contact with Mrs. Carter as her eyes filled with tears and she began to cry. Screwing up her face and covering her mouth to muffle her whimpers, she looked down at her feet to hide her sorrow from me. She grasped her tax return, her quarterly investments, and other miscellaneous spreadsheets in her hands so tightly that the veins and muscles in her arms bulged. Mr. Carter, seated beside her, put his arm around his wife to try to console her. He stared intently at her as she bent forward and put her hands over her face to try to hide her emotions. I then noticed that Mr. Carter was fighting back tears as well as his wife began to cry.

While this does happen occasionally when I meet with my clients, I never get used to seeing anyone cry. The feelings of sorrow and remorse always flood my thoughts and my emotions. I knew if I did not look away from the Carters now, I might begin to cry as well. I could tell this was the first time that the Carters had honestly looked at their current and future financial picture. They had just realized that their fortune, their dreams, their lifestyle, and their businesses that they had worked their entire lives to accumulate were about to come to an end simply because of the cost of their son's college education.

This was our fourth meeting together. In our prior meetings, we had briefly discussed their financial picture, and they knew things were bad. But this was the first time they saw accurate numbers with realistic projections and with their current accounts, which showed them a very frightening future. If they did not make drastic changes now to curb the overwhelming cost of their son's schooling, all of the money that they had ever saved would be gone.

I glanced out of my third floor office building to quickly get my thoughts together so that I would not be overcome with tears and so that

I could be as professional as possible. The sun was already setting on this late winter afternoon. "What a week this has been, and it's only Wednesday!" I whispered.

When I work with my clients, I try to put myself in their shoes and look at life from their prospective. I try to feel what they are feeling. I try to understand where they came from and where they would like to go. How did they end up in my office? What past experiences have they had with their money? Did they go to college? What was their major? Did they graduate? Did they have a good educational experience? Were they working in a different field than their college major? I also like to learn about their family heritage, their thoughts on college education, and their involvement in the community. I like to listen, to learn, and to appreciate my clients' stories so I can get a better insight into each person's life meaning and purpose. My clients are more than what their financial statement tells me, and their nonmaterial wealth is just as important to me as their material wealth. I know that if my services only dealt with the college search, money for college, and financial aid while ignoring the client as a human being, then my services would be devoid of any real enduring meaning or value.

I thought about Mr. Carter, who was 60 years old and had grown up in Connecticut. Mr. Carter's father had left him with a comfortable inheritance, and while most Americans would consider Mr. Carter's family to be wealthy, Mr. Carter's father made sure that he kept his son grounded as a child. Mr. Carter told me that his father made him and his brother wash their own clothes even though the family had maids throughout his childhood. He attended a prestigious private school in Connecticut, but then he decided to go to Georgia Tech for college because he had relatives in the south.

Mrs. Carter was six years younger than Mr. Carter at age 54. Unlike Mr. Carter, she grew up in a Midwest middle-class family with four younger siblings, an alcoholic father, and a mother who worked at the local factory in the evenings to pay the bills. Mrs. Carter attended public school her whole life, all the while dressing her younger siblings for school in the morning and often making dinner for the family at night while her mother worked. In the spirit of her mother, Mrs. Carter paid her own way through Georgia Tech by waiting tables.

She and Mr. Carter met during her sophomore year of college. After they graduated and were married, they became small business owners, but when the economy took a dive in early 2008, so did their businesses. When I first met Mr. Carter, he had the smell of alcohol on his breath, and, as I noticed how his normally carefree voice became muffled and stressed when the topic turned to finances, I wondered how long he had been drinking away his sorrows. Mrs. Carter, on the other hand, was well aware of their current financial troubles and knew they needed help immediately.

In spite of their troubles, the Carters were most proud of their two boys, Josh and Jim. Jim was already a junior in college, but Josh, the reason for our meeting that day, was just finishing his junior year at a private high school in Charlotte. At our first meeting several weeks ago, I found out that Josh had lost cell phone privileges because he was spending more time talking to his girlfriend than studying for his tests. However, Josh was still in the top 10% of his class and was maintaining a 4.1 GPA even with his tough advanced placement courses. Josh grew up as a big Georgia Tech fan, watching ball games almost every Saturday with his father. He wanted to go to one college and one college only even though he had never set foot on the campus of Georgia Tech. (And the public wonders why colleges spend so much of their budget on athletics! It is the greatest form of advertisement to high school students.)

I was suddenly brought back to the meeting when Mrs. Carter looked up from holding her head in her hands and said, "Ryan, what are we going to do? Josh really wants to go to an engineering school, and right now he only wants to attend Georgia Tech. Georgia Tech is an out-of-state public school, and it's probably going to cost us around $42,000 a year. I know Josh will be in school at least five years to become an engineer, so the total cost for just Josh to go to college will be around $200,000 to $250,000!

"We have been able to pay for Jim's college with our savings, but now I don't think we're going to be able to keep doing that. I still can't believe that Jim didn't get any scholarships or merit aid money to go to college!

He graduated second in his high school class of 450. He was a National Honors Society member, a good athlete, and an Eagle Scout." Mrs. Carter shook her head. "And you're telling me, based upon the expected family contribution calculation or how much the colleges think we can afford to pay, that we are not going to get any aid for Josh either!"

I could hear the frustration, desperation, and anger in Mrs. Carter's voice. She was not crying anymore, and she seemed to have cleared her mind enough to focus on the problem.

Mr. Carter took up where his wife left off. "As you know, Ryan, most of our wealth is in four stocks that I inherited from my father and a few mutual funds that my financial planner suggested. Since the market collapsed, the value of these accounts has fallen from over $1,000,000 to now just under $600,000. Even the 529 plan that Josh and Jim's grandparents started for them has dropped from $15,000 to only $12,000. (To me, that was astonishing, because they put $12,000 into the 529 plan almost seven years ago, and the 529 plan has lost money.) We have been drawing from our brokerage accounts for the last two years since both of our businesses need the cash and we need this money to live on to pay the bills. Our accounts are now down to around $450,000. At the rate we are withdrawing money from our accounts, we might not have anything left if things stay the way they are today! Helping our boys pay for college has always been one of our primary goals, but now I don't know if we can help them at all. What can you do to help us?"

"I can help you, and I will help you," I said to them. "I'm going to be your guide, your coach, your Sherpa, and your mentor through this college process. We don't have much time, but by the end of next May when Josh is walking across the stage to get his high school diploma, you will be extremely happy with what we have accomplished! Josh will be excited about going to a college that you know will be a good fit socially and academically. He will have a better idea if engineering is what he would like to study in college. He will have multiple colleges competing for him so that we can reduce the cost of college, and we will bring the college cost down to approximately what it costs to attend a state college in North Carolina. But we need to come up with a new plan to pay for Josh and Jim to attend college without you going broke."

I told them that they would need to follow my coaching and to implement my suggestions. (I can bring the horse to water, but I cannot make it drink!) "The system I am going to show you is easy to follow, and anyone can do it with the right guidance," I told them. "My business is about relationships and results. We might have a great relationship, but you will not achieve the results you expect if you do not follow my simple process. I have been working with families for almost 10 years, and on average we can help save $40,000 to $60,000 of college cost per child. And I will help you, too!"

What I told the Carters is exactly why I started this business back in 2003. While I was completing my MBA at the McColl School of Business at Queens University of Charlotte, I was working for General Electric. GE was kind enough to pay for my graduate degree, but I knew I did not want to continue with my job. By this time, I had worked for two large multinational corporations after graduating from the United States Merchant Marine Academy with a bachelor of science degree in marine engineering systems. I had traveled the world, and I had a job that paid well. However, I did not get up in the morning looking forward to going to work. I did not come home fulfilled or have a sense of accomplishment. I did not know what I wanted to do, but I knew it was not this. I knew there was more to life than money, and I also wanted to make a difference in society.

After leaving GE, I worked for a financial planning firm for a few years before I found my calling in life. During that time, I thought about my childhood and considered what my purpose in life should be. What was my mission going to be, and what were my goals? How could someone like me make a difference in such a big world? I also thought about what I liked to do and what would make a lasting impression. I thought about what I wanted my life to be like 3, 5, and 10 years from now.

I grew up in a small town called Raeford in Hoke County, North Carolina. Hoke County is primarily used by Fort Bragg military base for military training. Growing up right beside such a large military facility and having many military childhood friends and neighbors exposed me to many different cultures from around the world. Hoke County also has a very large Native American population, known as Lumbee Indians.

Speculation is that the Lumbee Indians were descendants of the "Lost Colony" that Sir Walter Raleigh established as the first English colony in the New World. It is not unusual to see many of these Lumbee Indians with blue European eyes or fair skin. Hoke County has a very large African-American population as well. In fact, I was a minority at every school I attended in Hoke County and Raeford. The Scotch-Irish established its roots in Raeford when the colonies were first being settled. Many of the families can trace their ancestors to this early European colonization. This unique mix of cultures made for an interesting melting pot in a small town in North Carolina.

Unfortunately, Hoke County is also one of the poorest counties in North Carolina. My father was born and reared in Hoke County, and he moved our family back to his hometown when I was three years old so that my brother and I could bond with our grandparents while they were still living. My mother was happy living in Cary, NC, where we lived, and she did not look forward to this move, as she had never lived in a small rural town.

Both of my parents were successful in their careers. My mother won many teaching awards in Charlotte and Cary, including teacher of the year. My father was an entrepreneur and a salesman at heart. At different times, he owned a men's clothing store, a night club, and several other businesses. But, like my mother, his greatest love was for education and books.

I have one brother, Chris, who is four years older than me. Chris is very intelligent, and he attended North Carolina State University to be an aeronautical engineer. I can remember my parents being so proud of my brother as he left for college. When Chris became a sophomore and junior in college, I noticed my parents had more frequent and heated discussions about how they were going to pay for Chris's college. While they tried to shield me from these conversations, I knew that they were struggling with this decision. Since my father worked on commission and my mother on a teacher's salary, they struggled to pay their bills because of the high cost of college.

This left a lasting impression on me! My parents did not tell me this, but I knew they did not know what they would do financially when I

went off to college. One of the reasons I attended the United States Merchant Marine Academy was to help my mother and father with college costs. It was a good decision! Years later, after graduating and working for companies like GE, I thought back to the decision and realized this was my calling in life: I wanted to help other middle-income Americans with college expenses. It all made perfect sense now! I could use my love of numbers that I learned as an engineer, the business knowledge from my MBA, the leadership training I received at the academy and as an officer in the Naval Reserves, my love for teaching and working with families, my experience as a financial planner, and my unique upbringing to work with families to help with the escalating costs of college through the pursuit of higher education.

Today, I have helped thousands of families protect their assets, increase their wealth, reduce their taxes, and get their college-bound students quality educations for less than they ever dreamed possible! I have been able to do this by learning what goes on behind closed doors at admissions offices and financial aid offices at colleges and universities. I know the business side of colleges and what colleges are afraid to tell you about financial aid. I know the insider information, the trade secrets, and the unique financial backroom discussions that the colleges and universities hide from the public. I will reveal what the colleges and universities do not want you to know.

Think of this like a game. The colleges know the rules of the game and how the game should be played. If this were basketball, they would be the NBA team and the referee, and right now you would be the junior varsity high school team because you do not know the rules of the game. Most parents believe they know the rules of the game because they have listened to a guidance counselor or visited a few colleges and listened to them speak. But trust me: You do not even know what you do not know! So when it comes time to play the game, the colleges will beat you every time. You pay retail and not wholesale for college costs every time.

Unfortunately, if you play the game this way, you ultimately pay the full cost for college, or the retail price. I am going to be your coach, and I am going to teach you what NOT to do so that you can learn the "rules of the game." Finally, you will learn the step-by-step guide to follow so that we can make this a fair game and pay wholesale college costs! Together as a team, we can obtain affordable, quality education for less than you ever dreamed possible.

Before I teach you the rules and how to play the game, I first need to teach you what not to do so that you can play this game correctly.

In *Education Pays,* the College Board stated that the expected earnings over the working lives of four-year college graduates add up to $800,000 more than the earnings of high school graduates. If you include college graduates who also earn a master's degree or doctorate, the lifetime earnings climb to $1,000,000 over a high school graduate. We can all agree that getting a college degree is important for our children socially and financially. However, the more college costs, the more money your child needs to earn to justify the cost of college and to justify this return on your investment. If parents don't play the game the right way and if the price of college continues to rise, at some future point in time, paying for college will not be worth it.

CHAPTER 2

Mistake #1: Depending on the College's Financial Aid Officer (FAO) for Unbiased Financial Advice

*"If you are sitting in a poker game and after 20 minutes
you do not know who the patsy is, then you're the patsy."*
– Warren Buffett

I'm going to share with you now and explain the really dumb, self-defeating, foolish, crazy, expensive, and time-wasting things that students and parents unwittingly do in the college process that will end up costing them thousands of dollars! Do you want to lose thousands if not hundreds of thousands of dollars? If you listen to my advice, you will save your family so much heartache, so much pain, so much time, and a lot of money! You will learn why parents who do the following always pay RETAIL and why the parents who follow my guidance pay WHOLESALE. You need make sure you are not one of the parents that will do one of the following so that you will not lose out on receiving great financial aid!

The college's financial aid administrators (FAA), financial aid counselors (FAC), or financial aid officers (FAO) are usually wonderful people who do a good job balancing the needs of families with the limitations of the college. Like any business, the colleges have financial and budgetary constraints that limit FAA generosity in dispersing financial aid.

I encourage every parent to get as much information as possible from as many resources as possible. However, you need to know the limitations and, more importantly, the basis of each of these resources. Many parents go to financial aid night at their local high schools and listen to a college financial aid officer. Well-meaning guidance counselors invite the FAO to give a talk on the various types of financial aid and how families qualify to get this money. Usually at the end of the meeting, the parents leave with the false impression that the financial aid award given by the colleges will leave them with no unmet or additional financial need. The guidance counselors wrongly assume that the FAO will put the best interest of the students before the college's own financial interest. *In reality, the FAO's main objective is to get the best student into his or her college for the least amount of financial aid!*

I know and work with many FAOs. I enjoy speaking with them, and they can be very helpful to families. However, you always need to remember that *the FAOs get paid by the college, and they always have the college's best interest in mind. Their loyalties are with their schools—not their applicants!* I do not mean to demonize the FAOs or the colleges' financial aid office or to imply any unnecessary blame. My intent is to bring to light the bias that does exist and that parents should be aware of.

In North Carolina, the colleges are very smart. They formed a nonprofit organization called the College Foundation of North Carolina (CFNC). CFNC is a partnership of the University of North Carolina General Administration, the NC Department of Public Instruction, the NC Community College System, and the NC Independent Colleges and Universities. CFNC is a free service of the State of North Carolina that tries to help students plan, apply, and pay for college. The CFNC Web site does have some very useful tools such as a career planning, electronic applications, and transcripts accepted by all 110 North Carolina colleges and universities, and it does give out some information on student financial aid and college affordability. They even have an "ask an expert" module that provides contact information for a CFNC financial aid specialist. Who do you think trains the expert?

Did you know if you take your tax return to the IRS, they will complete it for you for free? I am sure it will be done correctly, but I am not sure if you would get all the deductions. Likewise, if you depend on the colleges to give you financial advice, you will not receive unbiased information and I suspect not receive all the financial aid that you deserve. CFNC has the gall to send a letter to every student in North Carolina every year advising the family not to pay someone to complete the financial aid forms for them! I ask you, why would CFNC not want the families to get expert advice and help them with these forms knowing that the Department of Education states that 90% of the families applying for financial aid complete the forms wrong and are rejected? *Maybe it is because some of these experts (like me) have knowledge that they don't want parents to know!* CFNC goes to almost every public school in North Carolina to present financial aid nights that focus on completing the financial aid forms, and obviously families are still not getting the guidance they need—especially middle-class America. Most middle-class families wrongly assume they make too much income to get aid, so they don't apply for it.

Even if a so-called financial aid expert from a college or representative from an institution like CFNC comes to your child's high school, you need to remember that they get paid directly or indirectly by the colleges and that they always have the colleges' best interest in mind even if they are from a nonprofit organization. Their loyalties are with their schools—not their applicants! How can one college representative during a 60 minute presentation adequately address the complexity of the college financial aid system for every family and every college? It is impossible to do because every family's situation is different.

CHAPTER 3

Mistake #2: Relying on Your Accountant or CPA for College Financial Aid Advice

I love working with CPAs and accountants because we essentially do very similar jobs. I've had many CPAs and accountants become clients of mine after they hear my advice from other clients. They usually love what I do once they understand what I do. Most accountants and CPAs help put strategies in place to reduce your tax liability, and I put strategies in place to help my clients reduce the cost of college. They file federal 1040s and state taxes; I help my parents file the federal, state, and institutional financial aid forms. However, this is where the similarity of the two jobs ends.

Many CPAs and accountants have children who have gone to college, so they think they understand the financial aid process. Although they are experts in the tax code, finalizing tax returns, and tax reduction strategies, college financial strategies are completely different. There are many cases in which college aid strategies are the polar opposite of tax strategies. The implementation of some accounting and tax reduction strategies can cost you thousands of dollars in lost financial aid. Most accountants want you as a repeat customer next year when you need help with your tax return, and they don't want you to go to their competition down the road, so they may offer to complete your financial aid forms even if they hate preparing the financial aid forms.

While the IRS and your CPA are concerned about your finances all your life, the colleges are concerned about your finances for only four years (or longer if the student stays longer). The financial aid form and your federal taxes are linked, so it is very important to make sure your tax planning during the four years a student is in college is planned accordingly.

Also, because the financial aid formulas differ from the IRS formulas, the advice your CPA may give you for long-term tax reduction strategies may actually decrease your ability to get financial aid. For example, a CPA might advise a parent who owns a small business to shift income to his or her child to reduce the family's tax burden. From a CPA perspective, this is great advice because the CPA just saved the family some money in tax savings. From a college planning perspective, this might be devastating because this could potentially cause the family to decrease their aid opportunities and increase their cost of college!

There are some accountants and CPAs that have dedicated their practice and made it their business to learn the intricacies and the ins and outs of financial aid. Unfortunately, most parents don't know whether they are dealing with one of these experts or a novice beginner. I would start by looking for a CPA who is a member of the National Institute of Certified College Planners or the National College Advocacy Group. Also, make sure you ask your friends for referrals, and check the Better Business Bureau. You might also want to interview them by asking them a few questions:

1. How much do assets held in the child's name count on the FASFA form?

2. What is the asset protection allowance (APA), and how is it calculated?

3. Can you tell me the pros and cons of a Stafford Loan and a PLUS Loan?

4. Can you tell me about local state grants?

Do not ask a CPA if you qualify for financial aid. This question can only be answered after a detailed financial analysis on your current financial situation and the calculation of your expected family contribution (EFC) using the Free Application for Federal Student Aid (FAFSA) and the Financial Aid Profile form.

Any professional who does this for a living should know the name of the state grants offered by your state and the state's specific rules to qualify for this money. They should also know what the asset protection allowance is and how it is calculated. In addition, they should be able to let you know the pros and cons of all the different college loans. If a CPA cannot answer any of the above questions, he or she probably is not qualified. You don't want to be the guinea pig because most accountants and CPAs are paid by the hour, and they will gladly charge you as they try to learn.

CHAPTER 4

Mistake #3: Investing in a 529 Plan If Your Children Are in High School

Much like CPAs or accountants, there are a few financial planners that have dedicated their practice and made it their business to learn the intricacies and the ins and outs of financial aid. However, most have not. The media and financial planners encourage parents to start a 529 college savings plan. If your child is in high school, *do not start one!* There are better financial tools to save for college.

When I graduated from taking MBA classes, I knew I wanted to help people with their finances, so I started at a respected financial planning firm thinking that this was the best route I could take to help as many people as possible. I had a very lofty picture in mind of what financial planners did for a living and how they got paid. I thought that if I became a financial planner, I could gain inside knowledge of the financial markets on the closely held strategies that can make a big difference in someone's finances. I wanted to use this knowledge to spread this information to as many people as possible. As a recent MBA graduate who loved his financial classes, I thought that I would be surrounded by other MBAs, CPAs, and economists when I started my job. However, I quickly realized that the term "financial planner" had a very loose meaning. Someone can be a real estate agent one week and a financial planner a few weeks later. One is required to take more training as a licensed massage therapist than a financial planner. Bankers, brokers, life insurance salesmen, property-casualty insurance salesmen, and many other professions all consider themselves financial planners.

Before I started my financial planning career, I wanted to do research on every firm that was hiring financial planners. I decided the best way to do this was to go to each company, meet my potential bosses, and interview them.

The first company I chose to interview was a nationally known financial planning firm that everyone in America would know if I told you its name. I was scheduled to speak with the regional manager of the firm on a Tuesday morning. I drove to the wealthy part of downtown Charlotte, and, thinking I needed to make a good impression, I dressed in my best suit. I was a little nervous but very excited to see the movers and shakers in the financial industry. As I pulled my car into the parking lot, I was impressed with the high-rise office building where the company had its headquarters. There was marble everywhere: in the lobby, on the floors, and on the ceiling! This was definitely a "class A" office building, and it gave me a great first impression. The office building was located in a great part of town, and everyone looked very professional in their suit and ties.

The regional manager who greeted me at the receptionist desk was very young. He must have been in his mid to late thirties, and I was in my late twenties at the time. As I sat down in his large corner office, I asked him how he recruits new financial planners. He said, "Let me show you. We have some potential candidates interviewing today." We then proceeded down the hall to a small conference room filled with about 30 chairs facing a large TV on a rolling metal rack (the kind you would normally see in a library). He said, "We expect about 15 to 20 individuals to show up today, and we will start the meeting by showing them a video about financial planning and our company. I will then give a quick 15 minute talk about the wonderful benefits of working for the company, how the company will help them become a financial planner, and how they can be their own boss in just a few weeks." He then proceeded to give me the speech he was going to give the other people who would arrive later that day.

I then asked, "Out of the 20 or so people, how many do you hire?"

He said, "We hire them all!" as he grinned from ear to ear. I was taken aback by his response. I imagined it was going to be like my interview with General Electric in which no one was invited to an interview unless they had been thoroughly screened and many of their references checked. I had gone through grueling committee interviews in which four or five people sat behind a long desk and asked me question after question. But this was obviously nothing like what I had experienced in the past.

He then continued, "We will pay for you and every candidate to study and pass all the necessary testing and license requirements during the first few months. If you or any of the other candidates do not pass the test, your contract will be terminated. Once you pass the required licensing test, you will then need to maintain a minimum monthly quota of sales during the first year. If you or any of the other individuals do not meet the quota, you will not stay with us."

Now the truth hit me like a brick. I said, "So basically you try to get as many people through this door as possible and weed out the ones that can't make it because they can't pass the test or they can't make certain number of sales."

I then asked the regional manager how his financial planners get compensated. He said, "All my planners are compensated based on a commission by selling financial instruments like stocks, bonds, mutual funds, 529 plans, and so on. The company also gets paid a percentage of the commission to help pay for advertising, office space, copies, et cetera."

I thought to myself, "The planner only gets paid if he or she sells the client something." This was my first lesson in the world of financial planners: SALES ARE KING! I knew this was not the place for me! If this firm's only hiring criteria was to find as many people who could come through the door, then I knew this business model was not for me. It was a numbers game, and the training given to these "financial planners" was almost nonexistent. When I left the room and looked at all the people dressed very professionally wearing their dark suits and working in their elegant offices, I wondered how many of these individuals were former real estate agents, teachers, and salesmen that were now so-called financial experts after only a few weeks of training. With little training and the need to make commissions, you can see why 529 plans are recommend by most financial planners.

The second company I interviewed later that week was with a nationally recognized life insurance company. I had a bad feeling about this before I set foot in the door. Their office was just a few blocks away from the first company. I met with a well-dressed woman who had been selling life insurance her whole life. She was in her 50s, and she had a strong southern accent. She told me that her father had started the business many years ago. I learned that the hiring process was the same as the first company, but this company required you to sell a minimum number of life insurance policies each month. While you could sell another company's insurance policy to meet your monthly quota, you had to sell the proprietary insurance policies that this company owned. I kept thinking to myself, "If I am truly trying to help families, I don't want the pressure of having to sell insurance even if they do not need it." My second lesson in the world of financial planners was the same as the first lesson: SALES ARE KING! This was not the place for me either because of the conflict of interest. This concept needed to change in the industry. I don't blame the insurance brokers or agents because this is how they get paid. I blame the business model that encourages and gives incentives to push the selling of insurance. If you work with an insurance agent, do you think they would like for you to save for college in an insurance policy? While this might not be a bad choice, you need to make sure you see a variety of policies, not just the company they represent.

Next, I interviewed a brokerage firm that primarily sold stocks, bonds, and mutual funds. The planners got paid by the percentage of assets under management. Their minimum requirement for a potential financial planner was to amass a minimum of at least $1 million of assets under management during the first year. If you did not achieve the $1 million asset under management, your contract would not be renewed. In this business model, the financial planner got paid a percentage of the assets that he or she managed for a client. The percentage the planner got paid was based on a sliding scale with larger accounts paying a smaller percentage or smaller fee. While I liked the idea of the financial planner's commission being tied to performance of his or her recommendations, I knew this would also encourage planners to hold onto families' assets even if it was better for the clients to liquidate their portfolio. If you took away assets under management, you took away the planner's paycheck. No financial planner wants his or her paycheck to be reduced, so he or she certainly does not want you to remove any money from your portfolio. I also learned that while brokers are required to make recommendations that are suitable for their clients, they may recommend proprietary products in which they receive higher commissions and the firm pushes them to sell these investments. Brokers also have incentives to "churn" customer accounts by trading to make commission. To me, this is a conflict of interest that needs to be changed. I do not blame the brokers; I blame the business model. If this is how a broker gets paid, what do you expect? If you want to move your money out of a 529 plan, what would you expect a broker to say?

From this experience, I learned that most families end up investing their money on the recommendation of the adviser and do not spend the time researching the recommended investment of fees and commissions. If a family works with a broker, they are probably going to invest in stocks, mutual funds, wrap accounts, and 529 plans if they want to save for college. If a family decides to work with an investment adviser, then more than likely the family will invest in mutual funds and 529 plans for college. If a family works with an insurance agent, the family will probably invest in annuities or 529 plans to save for college. They all sell 529 plans, and that is what they are taught to sell if you want to save for college. Moreover, they usually sell "advisor-sold" 529 plans in which they receive a commission and sometimes higher fees than "direct-sold" 529 plans.

"Wall Street is the only place that people ride to work in a Rolls-Royce to get advice from those who take the subway."
– Warren Buffett

Many different businesspeople call themselves "financial planners." However, most Americans don't know the legal and regulatory differences between them. Also, most investors are confused about the different regulatory agencies that govern over investment advisors and brokers.

I ultimately decided to join a smaller financial planning firm that used the retainer business model. In this firm, the planner charged a client a flat fee for an agreed-upon level of service on an annual basis. The planners also received commission for selling financial products, but there was no quota or pressure to sell. I liked this business model the best because it avoided most conflicts of interest, but not all. I soon realized that financial planning and college planning are two completely different specialties.

Warren Buffett stated, *"Diversification is protection against ignorance. It makes very little sense if you know what you're doing."*

In my financial classes, I learned a great deal about the theory of diversification and asset allocation. Through diversification, you can eliminate unique risk, firm-specific risk, or diversifiable risk. Unfortunately, you cannot eliminate all risks through diversification because of market-wide risk. No amount of diversification can eliminate all risk. The theory behind diversification is that the more stocks in your portfolio, the less risk you have. Through efficient diversification, you can theoretically construct portfolios with the lowest possible risk for any given level of expected return.

Asset allocation is another tool financial planners use to reduce risk. The idea behind asset allocation is that investments are risky by themselves, but some financial tools (stocks, bonds, CDs, etc.) "zag" when other financial tools "zig," depending on the market conditions. By combining these different investments that don't move in lockstep with each other, you can reduce your risk of losing money. In theory, you can reduce the volatility of your investments by combining the right assets. If you meet with a financial planner, he or she will always talk about asset allocation and diversification.

One of my first clients as a financial planner was a middle-income family. The father had just retired from IBM and was enjoying his free time by going fishing and working around the house. His wife had two more years left before she could receive full retirement benefits from the school system. She taught middle school math. They had three boys, but the two older children were already married and moved away. Their youngest son was beginning his freshman year at a small private college. They had just enough money in their accounts to be able to pay for their youngest son's college costs with the help of financial aid they were receiving from the college.

When I was reviewing their plan with other financial planners in my firm, we all agreed that they should move their college money from a few stocks and CDs that they currently owned into a 529 college savings plan to take advantage of the tax benefits and to reduce their risk through diversification and asset allocation. They liked the idea of moving the money into the 529 plan so that they could pull money out of it every year to pay for their son's college education tax free. I helped them select the 529 I thought was best because of the low fees and the age-based asset allocation. We both liked the age-based asset allocation because it would automatically change as their son aged. The idea behind this is that as a child gets closer to college age, the investments move from riskier assets, like equity funds, to ones with more fixed incomes, like bond funds. Since this couple's son was already in college, all of their money was invested into bond funds inside the 529 college savings plan.

What a huge mistake this was! Not more than two years later, the father called me to tell me that their financial aid package had been reduced considerably. I was confused because I did not know why he was calling me about the reduction of his financial aid package. He explained to me that since he took money out of the 529 plan to pay for college last year, the college considered it an "outside resource" and they reduced their college aid by thousands of dollars! "Your advice to move my money into this 529 college plan has cost me THOUSANDS!" I did my best to explain to him that I had no idea that this would happen and that neither the company that sold the 529 plan nor the financial planning company told me this consequence.

The financial planning firm and my MBA classes taught me that the 529 money would not affect my clients' financial aid package. All the money in the 529 plan is considered a parent's resource on the FASFA. This means that it should only count 5.64% against need-based financial aid. So if a family invests $25,000 in a 529 plan, their need-based aid would be reduced by only $1,410. I was also taught that since most families have an "asset protection allowance" from $40,000 to $50,000, the formula would not even use this money in their formula.

While this is correct for Federal Student Aid money, or NEED-BASED AID, this statement is not correct with the colleges' own money. As I learned later when I became a college planner, colleges do not have to use the federal aid formula to give out institutional financial aid. This means that if the college is going to give out their money, they will probably not use the asset protection allowance and the federal formula that only counts 5.64% of 529 plans. The colleges are only obligated to use the Federal Student Aid (FSA) formula for federal money, not their own money. The college can use their own methodology or formula, which varies depending on the school. Most private colleges not only use the FASFA form, but they also use the College Scholarship Service (CSS) Profile form to determine a family's financial aid package. Some colleges even use their own financial aid form that is completely different from the FASFA form or the CSS Profile form. On the colleges' own financial aid forms, they can ask you what make and what model car you drive if they want. The colleges can choose which methodology or formula they want to use for their aid package. The 529 plans *can affect* the money a college will give out from their own money. They are **not required to count only 5.64% of the 529 or the asset allowance** *when they use their own formula to determine your expected family contribution (EFC)*. Colleges are required to use the asset allowance and the 5.64% formula only when they are calculating federal need-based aid. This is when I began to realize that there was a lot more to college planning than just 529 plans!

Not only had this family trusted me to have the best financial advice for them, but they also assumed I had the knowledge and expertise to know the financial aid ramifications of moving their money. I then realized that financial planning for retirement and college planning are completely different and that I needed to learn more. This was a wake-up call for me personally!

In the early 2000s, the market went down in value drastically and the 529 plan that this family recently purchased lost almost **30% of its value** in just a few months. This time I called the family to let them know about the account. When I called, I spoke with the mother. She was devastated to know that the money they had saved all their lives to pay for their son's college was not going to be enough to cover the cost of the last year of college for her son. She was going to have to keep working and push her retirement back at least another year or two to pay for her son's college because of my recommendation of a 529 plan.

That night I went home depressed and I felt like crying. I felt betrayed by the other financial planners that I asked for advice, by the financial planning firms that all recommend the 529 age-based investment, and by the 529 college plan itself. I kept thinking to myself, "How can this 529 plan, with its age-based asset allocation model that was invested in bonds and bond funds, lose money? It was diversified and it was allocated into so-called 'safe' investments. Almost 80% of their money was invested in bonds and bond funds. I was told that this investment could not lose value. How could it have lost almost 30% in just a few months? During the sharp market decline, the interest rates went up considerably, and the bond funds lost considerable value. Age-based diversification and asset allocation might have reduced this family's risk, but the 529 plan value lost almost two years of college education for this family!"

Not only did it lose its value, but the fees associated with the 529 were also extremely high. As I did more research on 529 plans, I was shocked by the fees and expenses. Most 529 plans only invest in mutual funds. I can remember in one of my finance classes, I was doing some research on the founder of the Vanguard Group, John Bogle. He basically invented the index mutual fund in order to keep fees low by reducing overhead and management fees that other mutual funds tend to charge.

SmartMoney Magazine recently interviewed Mr. Bogle, and he spoke about how most mutual fund investors must invest 100% of their money to invest in the fund, take 100% of the risk after the investment, but *shockingly only earn 20% return of the gains!* Surprisingly, 80% of the profits are taken by the mutual fund companies via fees and expenses. I would like to suggest that everyone read *A Random Walk Down Wall Street* by Burton Malikiel and *Stocks for the Long Run* by Jeremy Siegel. From reading these books and doing my own research, I have found that index fund buyers are likely to obtain results exceeding those of a typical fund manager whose fees and turnovers reduce yield. According to Vanguard, over the past decade only 28% of U.S. stock funds managed to beat the Wilshire 5000 Index.

At our next meeting, the father also told me about their recent conversation with their CPA. The CPA told them that the money they distributed from their **529 plan** to pay for college **was not completely tax free.** A percentage of the 529 money would be taxable because they were also taking the Lifetime Learning Credit. The family's "qualified education expenses" exceeded the amount of money withdrawn from the 529 plan to pay for college that year, so they had to pay taxes on this money.

In this example, this family withdrew approximately $12,000 from their 529 to pay $12,000 in college expenses. With the recommendation of their CPA, the family also claimed the Lifetime Learning Credit of approximately $2,000 (credit was based upon the family spending a maximum $10,000 towards college expenses). The tax law requires CPAs to subtract the $10,000 of college expenses used toward the Lifetime Learning Credit from the $12,000 this family withdrew from their 529 plan. Now this family had only $2,000 of "qualified education expenses" even though they withdrew $12,000 from their 529 plan.

I couldn't believe what he was telling me. I was told over and over that the main selling point of a 529 plan was the tax-free benefit when you pull money out to pay for college. I was now learning that this is not always the case. In many instances, families will have to pay some taxes when they withdraw money from the 529 plan and use the Lifetime Learning Credit or the Hope Learning Credit. (The IRS publication that explains this in more detail is at www.irs.gov/pub/irs-pdf/p970.pdf). I suddenly realized that college planning and financial planning is not the same and I needed to learn a lot more if I wanted to help families in the future with college planning, so I dedicated my entire business to learning as much as I could about the college aid game.

I believe most individuals in America need financial planning. We all need to plan more and save more. If you need a financial planner to help you achieve your goals, then please use one. Financial planners are very good at planning for your retirement. However, college planning takes different knowledge and different training than a typical financial planner.

College funding professionals are experts in financial aid that help families through the complex maze of the college funding process. If you needed brain surgery, you would not go to your primary doctor to have him or her perform the surgery. While your primary care physician is a doctor, he or she does not have the unique skills and knowledge to perform the surgery. If you're planning on college, why would you go to a financial planner that does not specialize in college planning?

If you do decide to work with a financial planner for college planning, I suggest you start by looking for one that is a member of the National

Institute of Certified College Planners (NICCP) or the National College Advocacy Group (NCAG). Make sure you interview them by asking them the same questions you would ask the CPA discussed in the previous section. Also, make sure you ask your friends for referrals and check the Better Business Bureau.

While working as a financial planner early in my career, I learned that 529 plans can hurt your college financial aid package. 529 plans are not safe because your account can go down in value, and the distributions are not always tax free because of the IRS tax laws. Everyone knows that 529 education plans can potentially have a few tax incentives for a few families, but those few tax incentives barely make up for the lack of return the investor actually receives because of account fees and expenses. Moreover, the tax incentives will not make up for the losses incurred because of market volatility. In 2009, most mutual fund companies started to raise their expenses and fees even higher. Obviously, this means more cash out of your college savings and less net return from the 529 plans and mutual funds. Why would anyone start one of these plans, especially in high school?

Most Americans do not have a college savings plan, so having one is better than not having one at all. So, if you have a 529 plan, you should congratulate yourself for being one of the few families who have saved for college.

If your child is in high school and you are thinking about where to save for college, I would suggest you not save in a 529 college savings plan. I think there are better ways to save for college than a 529 plan. If you want to learn more about where to invest your money for college, keep reading this book because I will guide you through the steps to make the best decision on where to invest your money.

CHAPTER 5

Mistake #4: Not Applying for "Early Action"

Knowing the difference between early admission, early read, early decision, early action, and early notification can have a huge impact on your finances and your student's college career.

Rolling admissions is a policy in which the college will inform the student of his or her status within a couple of weeks of the college receiving all the required application documents. These colleges tend to accept students until they have filled their quota.

Almost two-thirds of the country's colleges and universities have an early admissions program. However, the early admissions policies at these schools can be confusing because they vary so much. To make it even more complicated, different schools use similar language that can mean completely different things depending on the school. You have to know and understand the difference between early decision and early admissions at each school your child applies to. If you do not, it can end up costing you thousands of dollars in college aid!

By and large, you can separate early admissions programs at colleges and universities into either *early decision* (ED) or *early action* (EA). They both involve earlier application deadlines that come much earlier in the senior year than normal admissions deadlines. One of the biggest advantages of applying ED or EA is that your family will be notified of the colleges' admissions decisions much earlier in the year, some as early as November. Schools are pushing these early application deadlines earlier and earlier. A few years ago, the EA and ED deadline was November 30th. Then it was moved to November 15th and then to October 30th. I have seen some as early as October 15th this year, and it would not surprise me to see an October 1st deadline next year. Do you think colleges are moving the deadlines up to accommodate you, or do you think it benefits them the most?

Colleges are now accepting a higher percentage of the early admissions applicants than the normal application pool that they review later in the year. Our research has suggested that some schools admit as much as 50% of their freshman class from just the early applicants. This means that your child should apply early, because your chances of being accepted as an early admissions applicant are much better than they would be as a normal admissions candidate. Moreover, you will know much earlier if the colleges have accepted your child into the school.

But most importantly, you need to know that **early decision (ED) is binding** *(or at least it used to be).* In years past, ED meant that you could only apply to one college, and you were asked to forego all other college options. This means that if you applied to an ED school, you promised that you would attend that school and that school only if the school accepted your application. That was a big drawback for most families, because the student was obligated to attend the college no matter what the financial aid package looked like.

Most importantly, if a college knows you are obligated to go to their school, is there any incentive to give you a great financial aid award package? Of course not, because you did not make the college compete for your son or daughter. You have no leverage to negotiate a better award letter because the college knows you are going to their school. You have no other options, so ultimately you have no leverage! You will learn more about this later. (I am strictly referring to the colleges being able to use their own money to recruit students and not federal aid, which follows strict rules.)

Today some colleges still use this strict definition of ED. However, over the past couple of years, most colleges are now allowing students to withdraw their names after being accepted as ED and are NOT obligating the student to enroll if the family does not receive the financial aid package they need for their child to attend college. Most colleges want to tell you that you can withdraw your name after being accepted as ED, but it is true. For example, this past year a student of mine applied to Furman University using the Furman Early Decision Plan because Furman was by far her first choice in college, and together we built a plan that budgeted for this expected expense to attend Furman. The student applied to Furman by November 15th and completed the CSS Profile form by November 15th. She was accepted to Furman the week of December 15th. Furman sent the family the financial aid package before the end of December. The family decided to attend Furman because the financial aid package was what we expected based upon her test scores, her estimated financial aid award, and the EFC calculation earlier in the year. However, the student *could have* withdrawn her name if the financial aid package was not satisfactory.

In most cases, early decision today is different than it was five years ago. The ED does have its advantages:

1. It's easier to get into college because the admissions standards are slightly less rigorous.
2. Colleges haven't run out of aid money yet, so more is aid available.
3. Students are now NOT obligated to attend, so there is no risk of being locked into a poor award letter.
4. Colleges ARE competing for student in ED, so colleges have incentive to give good packages.

Even though applying ED has many advantages, my recommendation is that a family should apply ED only if they have pre-planned and budgeted a predetermined price for college, the college matches the budgeted price with financial aid, and it is by far the student's favorite school.

On the other hand, I highly recommend you always apply to colleges that have early admissions programs called **early action (EA)**. This is a nonbinding obligation, and you get the benefits of early notification if you have been accepted. You are also allowed to apply to as many schools as you want, even if you are accepted. By applying for early action, you are finding out early where your child has been accepted, you are creating competition between the colleges, and you are giving your family many college options. You now have some leverage (we will be discussing using leverage in later chapters and why leverage is so important). This only works if your child applies to colleges that want your son or daughter. Moreover, your son or daughter needs to apply to schools that he or she actually wants to attend. We will be discussing this more in later chapters as well, but for now, always apply early.

---

*Please avoid early read because I have seen drastic reduction in financial aid that was estimated to a family compared to the aid that was officially offered the family later in the year. Early read is when the colleges offer to calculate a financial aid package sometimes before the student has been accepted at the college and or right after they have been accepted. To perform this estimated aid calculation for you, the college requires you to give them your financial information at the beginning of the 12th grade and before the FASFA deadline. They encourage you to do this so that they can give you a very early idea of what your financial aid package might look like if the student does attend the college. I am not a big proponent of early read because the aid the colleges offer at this time is non-binding and can/does change when you receive the official financial aid award letter. The colleges usually will write on the bottom of the letter to the parent: **"This letter is a tentative estimate. No awards are official until you receive your Free Application for Federal Student Aid (FAFSA) data and issue a final award letter."** If the financial aid award can change, and the college still requires you to complete the FAFSA, it is a waste of time to complete the early read paperwork. You are better off completing the official financial aid forms early (not the early read form) and waiting for the official financial aid award letter from the colleges in the spring of the senior year. By skipping the official read, you will avoid confusion by eliminating potential changes from your estimated aid package from the early read letter and your official aid package from the official financial aid award letter sent in the spring. Moreover, by skipping the early read form, you eliminate any possible influence a family's financial information could play in the college admissions decision.

CHAPTER 6

Mistake #5: Believing That a Degree from a So-called "Prestigious College" Will Always Enhance Learning or Guarantee You a Better Career

This is a debate that has been discussed for years. I can tell you honestly that my first job after graduating from the United States Merchant Marine Academy was partly based on where I attended college. My first job was working for Sea-Land Inc., an international shipping company. They hired a lot of USMMA graduates to fill their open positions, and they had many graduates working for the company. Bank of America is famous for only hiring from a few colleges for their investment banking business. High-tech companies like Google and Microsoft carefully measure the intellectual abilities of potential employees because of the belief that having a high IQ makes a better employee.

Lewis Terman was a psychology professor at Stanford University. His forte, or specialty, was intelligence testing. He even developed the first IQ test. Terman studied gifted individuals all his life because he believed that the smartest and the brightest individuals would make the greatest contribution in society through advancement in science, art, government, education, and social welfare. In fact, he studied 250,000 elementary and high school students and selected only 1,470 children who scored between 140 to 200 on the IQ test. He called these young geniuses his "Termites." He believed that his Termites would change the world and that they were destined to be the elite of the United States. He tracked the male Termites all the way through adulthood. He divided the Termites into three groups: Group A was composed of those with true success stories: lawyers, physicians, engineers, and academics. Only 20% fell into Group A. Group B consisted of 60% of the population, and they performed "satisfactorily." The bottom, Group C, was judged to have not achieved success. They were bookkeepers and men with no jobs. Amazingly, one third of Group C became college dropouts and only a quarter had a high school diploma. Of the 150 in Group C, all of whom were considered to be a genius at one time, only eight earned graduate degrees. Obviously, IQ is not the only factor that helps determine success in life.

While the name on the diploma might get you in the door for an initial interview, it will not help you after that. It certainly will not increase your chances of long-term success in work or in life. Once you start working for a company and you have held one or two jobs, no one cares where you went to college. Your employment record will count more than where you went to college. Any hiring decisions will be based upon performance, evaluations, and references.

Alan Krueger wrote an interesting article on this subject and did an analysis to compare students who applied to and were accepted by comparable colleges. He surveyed 14,239 full-time workers and he found that earnings were not related to the selectivity of the college that students had attended. Whether the students attended a moderately selective or highly selective school made no difference in their average earnings. He basically found that a good student can get a good education almost anywhere.

If you look at the top executives from the nation's largest companies, you will find that becoming an executive has more to do with one's own motivation, ambition, and talents rather than where the executive received his or her undergraduate degree. Did you know that the majority of the CEOs and presidents of the biggest corporations did not attend an Ivy League school or another highly selective college? Most of them went to lesser-known private colleges and state schools.

Below is a good example of some very rich and famous individuals and where they attended college:

1. **Donald Trump** attended *Fordham University* and went on to attend Wharton School of Business.

2. **Oprah Winfrey** attended *Tennessee State University* with a degree in speech and drama.

3. **Adam Sandler** attended *New York University* and graduated with a fine arts degree in drama.

4. **Warren Buffet**t attended the *University of Nebraska* and then went on to get his master's degree in economics from *Columbia.*

5. **George Lucas** started studying anthropology at a *junior college* before transferring to the *University of California School of Cinematic Arts.*

6. **General Henry Hugh Shelton** acquired a textile degree from *North Carolina State University* while earning his Army commission through ROTC training.

Over the past few years, we have experienced some troubled economic times and troubled companies. Some of the CEOs and top managers of these troubled firms have graduated from the country's top universities. For example, John Thain, the former chairman and chief executive officer at Merrill Lynch, attended Massachusetts Institute of Technology for his undergraduate degree and Harvard Business School for his MBA. Let's not forget Richard Wagoner, who was in charge of GM as they went bankrupt. Mr. Wagoner attended Harvard Business School and Duke University. Goldman Sachs chairman and CEO Lloyd Blankfein graduated from Harvard University, and its president and co-chief operating officer attended the University of Chicago Booth School Of Business. Richard Fuld, who oversaw the bankruptcy of Lehman Brothers as chairman, received his MBA from NYU Stern School of Business. As you can see, attending a "named college" does not guarantee you success or the best education.

Are you still not convinced? Most people reason that any American who wins the Nobel Prize in science probably had a very high IQ, scored perfectly on his or her SAT or ACT, was embellished with scholarships, had a perfect GPA in school, and attended the best and most prestigious private universities in the United States. Did you know that in 2008, 27,462 of the very best and brightest seniors in the world applied to Harvard? Only 3,300 of these students scored a perfect 800 on the SAT math exam, and only 2,500 scored perfect on the critical reading section.

A few more than 3,300 were valedictorians at their respective high schools. Can you believe Harvard accepted only 1,600? To put it another way, they declined 93 out of every 100 applications they received. I think you will be surprised when I list where the Americans who have recently won the Nobel Prize in Medicine received their undergraduate degree:

Amherst College
Antioch College
Brown University
California Institute of Technology
Case Institute of Technology
Columbia University
DePauw University
Gettysburg College
Harvard University
Hamilton College
Holy Cross
Hunter College
Johns Hopkins University
Massachusetts Institute of Technology (MIT)
Union College, Kentucky
University of California Berkeley
University of Illinois
University of Minnesota
University of North Carolina
University of Notre Dame
University of Pennsylvania
University of Texas
University of Washington
Yale University

While this list has some very good colleges on it, I would argue that most of them do not represent where the best high school students in America apply. The question you should be asking yourself is, "Why are most of the colleges on the list not the so-called 'elite schools'?"

You are still not convinced? Okay, I will list the colleges of the 25 most recent American Nobel laureates in Chemistry:

Augsburg College
Berea College
Brigham Young University
City College of New York
Dartmouth College
Georgia Tech
Grinnell College
Harvard University (two laureates)
Hope College
Massachusetts Institute of Technology (MIT) (*two laureates*)
McGill University
Ohio Wesleyan University
Rice University
Rollins College, Florida
Stanford University
University of California Riverside
University of Dayton, Ohio
University of Florida
University of Massachusetts
University of Nebraska
University of Toronto
Washington State University

While Harvard and MIT both have more than one laureate, wouldn't you expect them to have more on this list since they are known to have the *very best and brightest students in the world*? Harvard, after all, is the wealthiest and most prestigious school! Moreover, the Ivy League and elite private colleges do not dominate the list, and they do not represent the majority of schools on the list. You can win a Nobel Prize if you attend the University of Minnesota, Harvard, or any college! Most families and students believe that Harvard is a better school than the University of Minnesota. That is true if you are looking at rankings and higher averages on the entrance exams. I hope you can see that rankings and reputation really do not matter.

Most parents will argue that Ivy League schools have more contacts than state and other private colleges that will help their children get jobs after college. All colleges have powerful alumni and many contacts. In his book *Harvard Schmarvard: Getting Beyond the Ivy League to the College That is Best for You*, Jay Mathews describes how he transferred from California's Occidental College to Harvard but found that the education he received at Occidental College paralleled or even surpassed his education at Harvard. Mr. Mathews calls the belief that big name schools make a difference in a child's future "Ivyholism." In his book, he has a comical 12-step process to rid yourself of "Ivyholism," an addiction that is not going away. Here are a few of those tips to help with "Ivyholism":

1. Getting into a brand-name school does not improve your life. Whether they attended Duke or the University of North Carolina at Appalachian, students with the character traits like persistence and charm do just as well financially 25 years after graduation.

2. Teaching and learning are often better in schools you never heard of.

3. All those smart kids rejected by brand-name schools make lesser-known colleges great. If a student was the valedictorian and scored perfectly on his or her SAT test but did not get into Harvard, Yale, or Princeton, then you must know that another college is getting a great kid that is very bright.

4. Why are all those foreign students happy to be at Cleveland State? The reason is that they have been taught before they came to the United States that it doesn't matter where you attend college in the United States because you will get a great education no matter where you attend.

5. This is NOT the most important moment in the applicant's life.

In May 2010, Adam Wheeler was a senior at Harvard University preparing for graduation. However, the 23-year-old was charged with identity fraud for submitting false transcripts and perfect SAT scores. Adam transferred to Harvard in 2007. On his Harvard application, Adam stated that he attended the prestigious Phillips Academy, scored perfect on his SAT, and attended two semesters at MIT. In reality, Adam graduated from a high school in Delaware, scored 1100 on his SAT, and attended Bowdoin College before transferring to Harvard.

The *Boston Globe* reported that Harvard found out about Adam's real identity when a professor was reviewing his application for the prestigious Rhodes and Fulbright Scholarships and noticed that Adam's work was plagiarized from another Harvard professor.

So Adam, a student who scored 1100 on his SAT and was kicked out of Bowdoin College for plagiarizing an essay, would have graduated from arguably the most prestigious university in America. Obviously, if the allegations are true, Adam Wheeler did an appalling act. But more surprising is how such an average student, in the eyes of Harvard admissions standards, could be on track to graduate from the most prestigious college in the United States!

What's the point, you ask? I believe that just because a student is trained at the country's top university does not guarantee a successful career. A college graduate's job and future earnings are unrelated to the selectivity of the college he or she attended. Your child's own motivation, ambition, and talents will determine his or her success and not where he or she will receive his or her degree. A good student can get a good education almost anywhere! To get the best education for your child, you need to find multiple colleges that match your child's academic strengths and interests. Getting into Big Name U or trying to hold up a family tradition is not the ultimate goal. The big picture or the ultimate goal is helping a young person with the path to success and happiness.

Parents, please do not live through your son or daughter. I know parents like to talk among themselves about their children's college search long before their children even think about college. Unfortunately, some parents put too much meaning on what their friends think about a college or what might impress their friends and not on what is best for their child.

Think of getting a degree like a bus ticket. The bus driver will let anyone on the bus if he or she has a ticket. Once the student gets on the bus, he or she can ride the bus to his or her future and let it take him or her anywhere he or she wants to go. If a student doesn't have the college degree, he or she will have to go to the back of the line, and more importantly he or she can't get on the bus. The driver does not care where people got the ticket or how they paid for the ticket. The bus driver just wants to know they have a ticket. Likewise, most companies don't really care where you received your degree.

Let's say you were the human resources director for a local business computer software company. You want to hire a new college graduate to fill a position. You have narrowed down the applicants to two recent graduates. Applicant #1 recently graduated from a nationally recognized university. He graduated in six years with a 2.0 grade point average. He did well when you interviewed him. Applicant #2 recently graduated in four years with honors from a small private college, and she has completed an internship with IBM and a co-op with a computer software company. These companies gave her raving letters of recommendation. She also interviewed very well. Whom would you hire? Most HR managers would hire Applicant #2, because she has shown that she can accomplish the task of graduating college, but more importantly the employer knows she can probably do the job as soon as she is hired because of the co-op and internship. It is not about the name on the diploma.

While working for GE and Sea-Land Inc., I interviewed many candidates and helped with the hiring decisions on several different occasions. Most companies spend a lot of time and money on hiring new employees because they know if they make a mistake, it will cost them much more in business, productivity, and ultimately a lot of wasted resources. The more proof you can give to an employer that you can do the job, the better. The National Association of Colleges and Employers (NACE) found that 95%of employers stated that a candidate's experience is a factor in hiring decisions. This survey also found that nearly half of the employers wanted new college graduates to have experience from internships or co-op programs.

Michael was one of those students a few years ago. Michael was in the top 10% of his high school graduating class and was a good athlete, a Boy Scout, a National Honors Society member, and a good person. Michael went to college to study aeronautical engineering. Michael wanted some extra spending money while in college, so he wanted to get a part-time job. Michael's parents were excited to hear that he wanted a job, and they knew he was getting excellent grades, so they thought it was a great idea. Michael took a job as a customer service representative for a large international airline carrier. Within a year, Michael had been promoted to a customer service manager position and was making good money. A few months later, he called his parents to let them know that he had been offered a high-paying manager's position at the airline's largest terminal in Los Angeles, CA, and he was postponing his education to pursue his career. As you can imagine, his parents were not happy and tried desperately to encourage Michael to finish his last year in college. Michael thought he would just transfer his college credits to a local college in Los Angeles and finish college while making more money than his parents. When Michael arrived at his new job, he fell in love with a wonderful girl. They decided to get married, and they traveled all over the world enjoying the perks of not having to pay for airplane tickets. Michael had not completed his college degree, but he thought he had plenty of time to complete a few more credits to earn his engineering degree. Michael and his wife soon had two beautiful children, and he continues to work for the airlines in California today.

I recently spoke with Michael, and he told me a sad but typical story. The airline wants to have Michael come work in their headquarters. They know Michael is very intelligent and very hardworking and could do a great job. The airline keeps reminding Michael that they are not allowed to hire him for any of these positions until he completes his college degree. They told him that they do not care what the degree is in, but it is company policy not to hire non-college graduates for these positions.

At a young age, Michael is stuck in his career with no chance of advancement. More importantly, he currently has a very good-paying job, but he is worried that if the airline decides to reduce the workforce, they might look at him first. He knows he cannot find another job that will pay as well as his current job without a college degree, so he is not able to change careers. He now has a very expensive mortgage to pay for and a family to provide for, and he does not have the time to finish his college degree because of his work schedule. Even if he did decide to go back to college to complete his degree, the requirements to get his degree have changed. Many of the credits that he has will no longer be accepted, so it will be like starting over from scratch.

Don't let this happen to your child. Get a degree, any degree, and your child can give the bus driver that ticket so he or she can take that bus to anyplace he or she wants to go!

CHAPTER 7

Mistake #6: Thinking That Not Scoring Well on the SAT or ACT Means a Less Successful Future

I first learned about Christopher Langan on the TV show 20/20 when Dr. Robert Novelly, a board-certified neuropsychologist, tested Langan's IQ and stated that Chris had the highest score in the 25 years of testing and that his score was off the charts. In 1999, *Esquire* magazine published a profile of Langan and called him "the smartest man in America." I learned later that Langan started talking at six months of age and taught himself to read by the time he was three years old. **Langan scored perfect on his SAT** and spent the majority of his time in high school independently teaching himself advanced math and physics. He was able to read and understand the concepts of *Principia Mathematica* at the age of 16.

He had dreamt of becoming a college professor and getting his PhD. Upon graduating from high school, Chris had scholarship offers from the University of Chicago and Reed College in Oregon. He decided to attend Reed College but lost his scholarship because his parents forgot to complete the financial aid paperwork. He left Reed College with all As for the first semester and all Fs the second because he didn't take his final exams.

He went back home to Montana to study at Montana State University. He left Montana State because he felt he could do without college and the higher-education system. He stated that he was too bored to listen to his teachers.

Over the next 20 years, he took a run of labor-intensive jobs such as a construction worker, forest service firefighter, cowboy, and many others. He finally settled in Long Island, NY, and he became a bouncer at a bar for over 20 years. Today, Chris Langan is married and lives in rural Missouri on a horse farm.

Chris is certainly a very smart man; he has a higher IQ than Albert Einstein and *scored perfect on his SAT.* However, many would argue that even with such unique talent and intellect, his contributions to society so far have been very small. Chris Langan is a perfect example of why it is so important to pick a college that is a good fit for your child and not pick a college based upon Big Name U. He also exemplifies that just because a student does well on his or her SAT, this does not guarantee success.

Malcolm Gladwell wrote about Chris Langan in his book *Outliers.* He also wrote in his book about the University of Michigan law school and how it uses affirmative action to assist students with lesser test scores to get into their law school. Approximately 10% of the students at the University of Michigan each year would fall in this category of relaxed admissions standards. If they did not use the relaxed admissions standards of test scores, only about 3% of minorities would represent the college. Consequently, those affirmative action students do receive lower grades in law school. Affirmative action remains controversial for the many of the elite U.S. educational institutions, because affirmative action leads them to admit so-called less qualified students.

Not many years ago, the University of Michigan took a close look at the law school's affirmative action students. They wanted to know how well they did once they left the college. They wanted to see how they fared in the real world, their progress in their career, what contributions to society they had achieved, if they had received any honors or awards, and everything else the college would consider real-world success. The college stated before the results that they only expected to find half of the students to compare favorably with the non-affirmative action graduates. They were completely surprised because they found no difference or discrepancy between the two sets of law school graduates. They were just as successful! **Being a success in college and when you graduate from college has less to do about how well you did on the SAT and ACT and more about your personal drive and determination.**

Not all colleges are recruiting the same type of student. Moreover, not all colleges have the same mission. For example, DePaul University states the following on its Web site:

"DePaul invites to its programs of study students from across the nation. Originally founded for students from the greater Chicago area, and still serving them predominantly, DePaul continues its commitment to the *education of first generation college students*, especially those from the diverse cultural and ethnic groups in the metropolitan area. Admission standards for all degree programs are selective or highly selective. In admitting students the university places greatest weight on intellectual potential and academic achievement. It seeks diversity in students' special talents, qualities, interests, and socio-economic background."

Now let's take a look at the mission statement of the California Institute of Technology (CalTech):

"The mission of the California Institute of Technology is to expand human knowledge and benefit society through research integrated with education. We investigate the most challenging, fundamental problems in science and technology in a singularly collegial, interdisciplinary atmosphere, while educating outstanding students to become creative members of society."

As you can see, the student that DePaul University would like to recruit and the student that CalTech would like to recruit are probably not the same because they have different missions.

Not all colleges are looking for a student who has a perfect SAT score, is captain of the football team, and won class president. Some colleges are even looking for students who received B and C grades in high school because they offer small classes with a lot of one-on-one time with the professor, which will ultimately enrich and empower the students. I highly recommend reading the book *Colleges That Change Lives: 40 Schools That Will Change the Way You Think About College* by Loren Pope. In her book, she talks about some of these colleges and universities.

Not every college will put the same emphasis and weight on the SAT and ACT. The National Center for Fair and Open Testing (FairTest) keeps an updated list of colleges and universities that deemphasize the use of standardize test. When you go on your college visits, you should ask two questions.

1. What are your most important admissions criteria?
2. How are the admissions criteria ranked?

By asking these questions, you will know if a college will look at a student's high school transcript first, the student's GPA, or the SAT score. You might find out that the school will look at a student's SAT score first and then class rank. You certainly will want to find out how much the standardize test weighs on admissions decisions. In addition, you also might find out that a college puts a great deal of emphasis on extracurricular activities and community service. This will help you know what to emphasize or highlight on your application or essay and if the school will be a good fit for your student.

Generally, private colleges do not put as much emphasis on the standardize test as the large state colleges and universities. I found a graph in an SAT prep book that shows how much weighting a large state university vs. a small private college has on the standardized test:

Large, State University

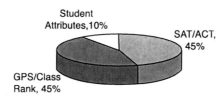

Small, Private Liberal Arts College

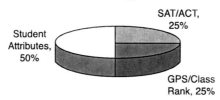

As you can see from the graphs, the large state university places almost 45% weighting on the standardized test, while the small private college only places 25% weighting on the standardized test. You are probably thinking, "Why would a large state college put so much weighting on the standardized test?" In most cases, it is because the large state universities receive a large volume of applicants each year and they need some way to narrow down and filter the applications to a reasonable level. By using the SAT score, they are able to eliminate some students who they think will not qualify.

I don't want you to downplay the importance of the standardized test scores. Colleges like to downplay their importance; however, the test scores matter more than they say. If you take the test and don't do well, you need to know that you can still go to a great college and get a great education! More importantly, no one cares what you scored on the SAT and ACT when you are in the real world. In fact, the University of Michigan found no difference in income or advancement among the law graduates with smaller standardized test scores and law graduates with higher tests scores. Being a success when you graduate from college has less to do with how well you did on the SAT and ACT and more about your personal drive and determination.

Getting a college degree is extremely important and should be a student's number one goal. This is the minimum that a student and his or her parents should try to achieve. *The College Board found that 40% of the students enrolled in four-year institutions never earned a degree.*

For an admissions officer or an enrollment manager at a college, retention of a student is very important. From the college's point of view, a student terminating his or her college education and a student transferring to another college is the same: they have lost a paying customer. Don't be fooled. Colleges do use SAT scores to help them decide which students will likely come back year after year, and this helps the college with their admissions policies and practices. The College Board states that the colleges should use the SAT to predict first year grades at a college and not long-term success.

Don't compare your SAT or ACT scores with other students. Most students like to compare and look at only SAT and ACT score ranges of the colleges. Right now don't worry so much about what other students achieved on the test.

I was not a great test taker, and a lot of my students are not great test takers. That is okay because not all colleges put as much weight on the standardized test and not all colleges are recruiting the same type of student. Conversely, just because your student did do well on the standardized test and has a high IQ, that does not equate to a great college experience or success in life after college. The most important factor is finding the right college "fit!"

CHAPTER 8

Mistake #7: Imagining the Financial Aid Process Is Fair

"The golden rule is he who makes the gold, makes the rule."
– Wizard of Id comic strip

I recently worked with a family that had a stock portfolio worth over $1 million dollars and a rental home worth $1 million dollars. This family received a full ride worth $33,000 a year in tuition including a $3,500 need-based grant. Is this fair? No, but nothing in life is fair, especially college admissions or college financial aid. Is this legal? Absolutely! For this family, and all the families I work with, we follow the legal loopholes that the Department of Education allows us to use to legally and ethically get as much aid as possible.

Much like your CPA or accountant will try to save you money by helping you implement strategies to reduce your tax burden, this system of checks and balances has worked for many years with the IRS and the CPAs as long as both sides follow the rules and guidelines. This system of checks and balances works well for the Department of Education, too. I parallel the work of a CPA in this instance because I also help my families reduce their burden to pay for college by implementing proven strategies that reduce the cost of college.

Some parents ask: Is this fair to everyone? I even had a parent tell me that it does not seem right if they get money from a college because they implement these strategies and another needy child does not get the money.

In 2007 and in 2008, Congress reviewed the financial aid polices of many of the top universities and their lack of use of their multibillion-dollar endowment funds. Some members of Congress wanted to make the colleges and universities spend at *least* 5% of their endowment because the colleges were not spending the money. In fact, they were making a lot of money through investments and tax breaks. One hundred and thirty-six of the largest grossing colleges and universities had to submit detailed information about their financial aid and endowment spending policies to the Finance Committee. Senator Charles Grassley (R-Iowa) stated that college endowments have ballooned over the years and, more importantly, so has college tuition and college presidents' salaries.

Even worse, some of the colleges and universities use the endowment money on capital projects, like buildings, instead of helping parents reduce the cost of college. For example, Princeton recently constructed a new dorm that cost approximately $120 million. To put this in perspective, it cost $35,000 per bed! Are these students staying in a resort or going to college? You can see why many colleges are being accused of wasteful spending, careless management, and overzealous expansion. Some colleges are in financial trouble right now, but I would argue that it is mostly their own doing. Many would say that the colleges will be better off in the long run because now they can focus on reducing waste, trimming fat, and cutting excess spending. However, you should not have to pay for the sloppy management, wasteful expenditures, and bad decisions of the colleges and universities.

The financial aid system is out of date, and as college costs continue to skyrocket, the colleges are ultimately failing their primary mission. The financial aid system was designed to expand access to a college degree to those who need it most. Unfortunately, our government continues to put more money into this flawed system, and the colleges are in no hurry to change the system's flaws.

The president of the college and financial aid officer (FAO) are responsible for increasing net tuition revenue. In addition, you need to understand that the job of the FAO is to get the best student into the college for the least amount of money. The FAO will do this by not only looking at your income and assets, but also demanding intimate facts about your personal life such as: make and model of the car you drive, marital status, student driver's license, how much you have in your retirement accounts, how much equity you have in your home, recent medical problems, and the student's outside scholarships, to name just a few. The

FAO is much more intrusive than any IRS agent. Remember, the FAO's job is to get the best student into the college for the least amount of money. In other words, they want more parents to pay the full cost of college. Your job is to know the rules and use this to your advantage.

Do you pay taxes? If you do, then you have already contributed to many financial aid funds for most of your adult life. A percentage of the taxes that you pay goes to the Federal Student Aid programs and to the state colleges and universities for state-specific grants. You probably didn't realize that you have been paying all these years so your son or daughter can attend college. Now is when you need to ask to use this money to help pay college costs, so don't be embarrassed.

CHAPTER 9

Mistake #8: Believing That You Should Not Apply to Private Colleges Because of the Sticker Price

The cost of attendance (COA) of a college is the estimated cost of completing a full year of college. Colleges arrive at this number by adding the cost of tuition, room and board, miscellaneous fees, books, transportation cost, and personal supplies. The average COA of a state college in the United States is approximately $14,500. The average COA for a private college is approximately $33,000, and the average COA for an elite college is over $50,000 a year.

In these tough economic times, where do you think most parents encourage their children to apply: state colleges or private colleges? Most parents I work with encourage their students to apply only to state colleges because they only see COA price and not the final price. They look a $15,000 state school and a $30,000 private college, and most parents will not even visit the private college. If most parents are encouraging their students to apply to state schools, do you think the state colleges are getting a lot of applications? In fact, they are receiving a record number of applications, and acceptance rates are dropping.

The University of Virginia received 22,516 applications this year, and their acceptance rate for in-state students was 42.4%. That was 677 more than last year, and they only accepted 6,907 students in 2010.

Last fall, the University of North Carolina received a record 23,047 applications. It was a *21% increase over the past five years!*

Unfortunately, the majority of the state schools depend on the state government for their funding. With tax revenue declining over the last few years, most of the state colleges are tightening their belts and reducing aid. In the College Board report "College Trends in College Pricing 2009," the state government appropriation per student declined by 5.7% in 2008-2009 in inflation-adjusted dollars. In addition, the state tax appropriations per student during this same time frame were 12% lower than a just a decade ago.

Figure 10a: Annual Percentage Changes in State Tax Appropriations for Higher Education per Public Full-Time Equivalent (FTE) Student and in Tuition and Fees at Public Four-Year Institutions in Constant 2008 Dollars, 1978-79 to 2008-09

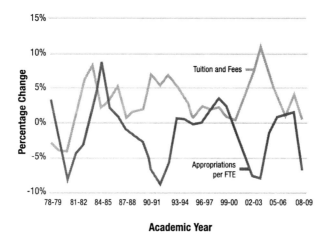

Percentage changes are in constant dollars. The 0% line corresponds to dollar increases consistent with the overall rate of inflation in consumer prices. Negative changes indicate declines in inflation-adjusted amounts.

With the record number of applications and with tax revenue being down, the state colleges' ability to give a lot of financial assistance has been dramatically reduced, and the competition for these dollars has increased significantly.

If you play the college game the right way and follow my suggestions, in many cases a private college can be about the same cost or cheaper than a public state college. Let me give you an example of what I mean. Let's look at the total cost to attend a $15,000 state college. The COA to attend the college is $15,000 a year. The family's expected family contribution (EFC), or the amount of money the college and/or the government expects this family to pay, is $5,000. (We will be covering this need-based aid formula later in the book.)

COA:	$15,000
EFC:	- $5,000
Financial Need:	$10,000

Out of this $10,000 of financial need, most state schools do not meet the entire amount. In this example, let's say the state college will meet 30% of the financial need, leaving a 70% "gap" that the state college will not meet. This means that the family will somehow need to come up with money to cover the gap.

Financial Need:	$10,000
Need Meet (30%):	$3,000
Gap (70%):	$7,000

Moreover, of the 30% ($3,000) of need met aid given by the state school, only half of it will be in "gift aid," or free money ($1,500 gift aid), and the other half will be in loans or work study ($1,500 in loans). The family will have to pay back the loans and work study, so we need to add this amount into our total cost of college. Now let's calculate the net cost of college for this $15,000 state school:

EFC:	$5,000
Gap:	$7,000
Loans:	$1,500
Total Cost:	$13,500

Let's compare the total cost of a private college that has a COA that is twice as much as the state school. The family's EFC is the same at $5,000 a year, so their financial need calculation would look like this:

COA:	$30,000
EFC:	- $5,000
Financial Need:	$25,000

Where the state colleges are only meeting 30% of this need, the private colleges tend to meet a greater percentage. In this example, let's use 100% so that there is no gap.

Financial Need:	$25,000
Need Meet (100%):	$25,000
Gap (0%):	$0

More importantly, private colleges also tend to meet the majority of a family's financial need with "gift aid" or free money. In this example, let's use 80% of the family's financial need as met with gift aid ($20,000 in gift aid) and only 20% with loans and work study ($5,000 in loans). Now let's calculate the true cost of college for this $30,000 private school:

EFC:	$5,000
Gap:	$0,000
Loans:	$5,000
Total Cost	$10,000

It would cost the family $13,500 to attend the state school and only $10,000 to attend the private college!

Most parents make the mistake of looking only at the COA and not the final price when comparing colleges, and so they push their students to apply only to state schools because they believe this will be the cheaper choice. The final price in this example was $13,500 to attend the state college or $10,000 for the student to attend the private college. Don't be intimidated by the sticker price of the college.

CHAPTER 10

Mistake #9: Believing That Parent PLUS Loans Are a Good Way to Pay for College

More than likely your family will have some type of college loan. While college loans are not the most exciting part of the college experience, you must know the basics of student loans, because most colleges will give a family some form of loan included in their financial aid award package. The most common forms of aid you will see on the financial aid award package are the Federal Stafford Loan and the Parent PLUS Loan.

Below is a good example of what you might see on a financial aid award letter:

Awards	Fall	Spring	Total
Scholarship	2,000	2,000	4,000
Subsidized Loan	1,750	1,750	3,500
Unsubsidized Loan	1,000	1,000	2,000
PLUS Loan	*7,500*	*7,500*	*15,000*
Total Awards		**$24,500**	

The Federal Direct Subsidized Loan, the Federal Direct Unsubsidized Loan, and the Parent PLUS Loan all are considered an "award" from the college's point of view.

The Parent PLUS Loan is used for any unmet need or "gap." This unmet need is the difference between the cost of the college and the family's ability to pay.

At almost every college, the federal, state, and loan company information and Web sites will suggest that you use the federal loans because they offer fixed, low interest rates. They include Perkins, Stafford, Parent PLUS, and Graduate PLUS Loans.

Student loans can be categorized into two groups: federal loans and private loans. Federal loans include Perkins, Stafford, Parent PLUS, and Graduate PLUS Loans. All except the Parent PLUS Loan require you to complete the FASFA (Free Application for Federal Student Aid).

Current Stafford Loans are fixed interest rates loans with limited borrowing limits. The Stafford Loan can be subsidized or unsubsidized.

The **Subsidized Stafford Loan** is in the student's name and is a *need-based loan* in which the federal government pays the interest on the loan until six months after the student leaves college. After July 1, 2010, the interest rate is fixed at 4.5% for undergraduate students and 6.8% for graduate students.

The amounts the student can borrow vary for each year of school and are as follows:

Undergraduate Year	Loan Amount
1st year	$ 3,500
2nd year	$ 4,500
3rd and 4th year	$ 5,500
5th year if needed	$ 5,500

The aggregate limit is $23,000 in subsidized loans.

In 2007, the College Cost Reduction and Access Act changed the interest rates on the Subsidized Stafford Loans. Any Subsidized Stafford Loans that pay out after July 1, 2010 and before July 1, 2011 will have a fixed interest rate of 4.5%, and any loans disbursed after July 1, 2011 and before July 1, 2012 will have a fixed interest rate of 3.4%.

The **Unsubsidized Stafford Loan** is *not a need-based loan*, and interest starts to accrue on the loan immediately. A student can request not to make interest payments while in school and add this interest to the principal of the loan. Most parents and students do request for "interest capitalization" of their loan so that they do not have to make interest payments while in school.

The amounts the student can borrow vary for each year of school, and the total undergraduate Stafford Loans (subsidized and unsubsidized) cannot be more than $31,000 for a dependent student.

Undergraduate Year	Loan Amount
1st year	$ 5,500
2nd year	$ 6,500
3rd and 4th year	$ 7,500 per year
5th year	$ 4,000

The lifetime limit is $31,000 (up to $23,000 may be subsidized) for undergraduate dependent student.

* If you are a dependent student whose parents are unable to get a PLUS Loan or an independent undergraduate student, you may be eligible for additional student loans. These loans are in addition to any Federal Subsidized or Unsubsidized Stafford Loan amounts received and are unsubsidized.

The total undergraduate Stafford Loans (subsidized and unsubsidized) cannot exceed $31,000 for a dependent student or $57,500 for an independent student. Dependent students are, in general, students under the age of 24 who are not married and have no dependents. If the parents of a dependent student are unable to obtain a PLUS Loan, the student becomes eligible for independent loan amounts.

The **Federal Perkins Loan** is a *need-based loan*, and it is in the student's name. The Federal Capital Contribution (FCC) provides funds to the approximately 1,800 institutions that participate in the Perkins Loan program. It is administered by the U.S. Department of Education. The colleges determine the amount of the loan, and the loans are made from a revolving loan fund in which the FCC matches the contributions from the colleges. Unfortunately, there have been no new FCC funds for several years, so the colleges make new loans as existing borrowers pay back existing Perkins loans. The limits can range up to $5,500 per year for undergraduate students and up to $8,000 for graduate students. The federal government pays the interest on the loan until nine months after the student leaves school, at which time payments on the loan begin. The interest rate is fixed at 4.5% for undergraduate students for the 2010–2011 school year and decreases to 3.4% for new loans originated in 2011-2012. The interest rate will increase back to 6.8% in 2012-2013. Payments can be deferred for students going back to school or in certain cases of hardship.

The **Federal Parent Loan for Undergraduate Students (PLUS)** is in the parent's name, and it is not a need-based or merit-based loan. Parents may borrow up to the full cost of their children's education.

Most parents will qualify for this loan. Conversely, only one denial from a parent is sufficient to qualify the family for an additional $4,000 to $5,000 in the Unsubsidized Stafford Loan as long as the other parent has not applied and been approved for a loan. If the parent later reapplies for a loan and is approved, the student will lose increased limits for the rest of the year (student can keep what has already been disbursed).

If a student receives any other financial aid, the parent can borrow PLUS for the cost of attendance less the aid received. The interest rate is fixed at 7.9% in 2010, and you pay this loan monthly on a 10 year term. Most parents pay back this loan making monthly interest and principal payments within a few months of taking the loans. Because of the Ensuring Continued Access to Student Loans Act of 2008, parents also have the repayment options of:

a) Making interest only payments while the student is in college and start full principal and interest payments after the student leaves school, or

b) Deferring the payments until six months after the students leaves school.

What makes this unusual is that the parents must start making payments on the PLUS Loan *before* they have the option to defer payments or only pay interests on the loan while the student is in school.

I receive at least one phone call a week from parents who went to one or my workshops but decided not to come meet with me personally because they thought they knew how to play the game but now find themselves in financial trouble. Most of the time, the parents have taken out Parent PLUS Loans and have obligated themselves to pay back these loans.

For example, this week I spoke with Carol Jones. She attended my college planning workshop at a local high school a few years ago but decided not to come see me personally to see if I could help their family before their first child went to college. At the time of the workshop, her oldest son was a senior in high school. Her son is now a senior in college and her daughter is a senior in high school. On the phone, she sounded in desperate need of help because she did not know how she was going to be able to afford to pay for her second child to attend college in a few months.

I then asked her how she was currently paying for her older child's college cost. She told me that he did receive a small scholarship his freshman year, and her son did take an Unsubsidized Stafford Loan. However, she had to take out a Parent PLUS Loan each year to make up for the "gap" to cover the rest of the college bill. The first year she accepted a $12,000 Parent PLUS Loan, the second year she took out another loan for approximately $13,000, the third year she had to take out a $14,000 loan, and this year she had to take out a $15,000 Parent PLUS Loan. At the time she took out the loans, the fixed interest rate for the Parent PLUS Loans in the FFEL program was set by the U.S. government at 8.5%. When she took out the loans, she agreed to pay back the loan monthly on a 10 year term by paying interest and principal.

During her son's freshman year at college, she said the Parent PLUS Loan worked great because, borrowing $12,000 at 8.5% for 10 years, she could easily afford the monthly payment of $149. The second year she said it got very tough because when she borrowed the $13,000 Parent PLUS Loan, the payment was $161 for this loan in addition to the $149 for the previous year's loan, totaling to a monthly payment of $310. The third year she was financially stretched because she had to add an additional payment of $174 per month for the $14,000 Parent PLUS Loan, which brought up her total monthly payment to $484 per month. Now with yet another $15,000 PLUS Loan for her son's senior year, she said her budget was stretched because now she is obligated to pay $670 per month.

While she was talking, I inputted these numbers in a spreadsheet so I could e-mail my findings for her. I wanted her to see how this might turn out if she continues to try to pay for her daughter's college using the Parent PLUS Loan.

Let's assume that next year her daughter goes to a similar college as her son, so this mother would need to come up with $16,000 for her freshman year of college, $17,000 her sophomore year, $18,000 her junior year, and $19,000 her senior year. (You have to assume college will increase its prices each year.) Let's also assume that the mother will continue to take out a Parent PLUS Loan at a new interest rate of 7.9%. Next year her monthly payment will increase to $863. Her monthly PLUS Loan payment will then increase to $1,068 her daughter's sophomore year and to $1,286 her junior year. The monthly payment will maximize to $1,515 her senior year!

As you can see from the below chart, she would continue to pay off this loan until she reaches 65 years of age. At $1,515 per month, that was $500 more than her mortgage.

Year	Parent's Age	Student 1	Student 2	TOTAL COST	MONTHLY TOTAL LOAN COST	YEARLY TOTAL LOAN COST
0	49	$12,000		$12,000	$149	$1,934
1	59	$13,000		$13,000	$310	$4,030
2	51	$14,000		$14,000	$484	$6,286
3	52	$15,000		$15,000	$670	$8,704
4	53		$16,000	$16,000	$863	$11,216
5	54		$17,000	$17,000	$1,068	$13,886
6	55		$18,000	$18,000	$1,286	$16,713
7	56		$19,000	$19,000	$1,515	$19,697
8	57			$0	$1,515	$19,697
9	58			$0	$1,515	$19,697
10	59			$0	$1,366	$17,762
11	60			$0	$1,205	$15,667
12	61			$0	$1,032	$13,411
13	62			$0	$846	$10,993
14	63			$0	$652	$8,480
15	64			$0	$447	$5,810
16	65			$0	$230	$2,984
17	66			$0	$0	$0
					$0	$0
interest rate:		8.5	7.9		$0	$0
						$196,966

Of course she could not afford this monthly payment, and like most parents, she did not calculate the monthly cost for the entire cost of college. Be careful when colleges, loan companies, state agencies, and other associations encourage you to take out federal loans first. I do agree that you should use the Stafford Loans and Perkins Loans, but I think you really need to be careful when you choose the Parent PLUS Loan, because you could easily obligate yourself to financial disaster paying for college!

CHAPTER 11

Mistake #10: Failing to Know the Difference Between "Expected Family Contribution" vs. "Your Ability To Pay"

Most parents know that the expected family contribution (EFC) is the minimum amount of money that a family is expected to contribute to the student's education at most colleges. It is determined by the FAFSA form using the Federal Methodology (FM), the CSS Profile form using the Institutional Methodology (IM), or the college's own financial aid form. The EFC is used to determine the student's eligibility for need-based financial aid such as Pell Grants, Perkins Loans, Federal Work-study, the Supplemental Educational Opportunity Grant (SEOG), and other need-based aid. All colleges require the FAFSA form to be completed.

While the federal government determines your EFC using the FAFSA form, *the colleges determine your EFC* using the CSS Profile form. These colleges do not believe that the EFC calculated by the FAFSA form is an accurate depiction of a family's financial condition, so they require a family to complete the more detailed CSS Profile form or the college's own financial aid form. The CSS Profile form is much longer and much more complicated than the FAFSA form. However, the numbers on the FAFSA form need to be consistent with the numbers on the CSS Profile form.

Without going line by line, I will briefly list some of the notable differences on the forms. You will find some of the following on the FAFSA form:

1. Student assets are assessed at 35% per year.
2. Has an Income Protection Allowance (IPA), or amount of income exempt from the financial aid formula

3. Excludes your personal home equity
4. Excludes retirement accounts
5. Student-owned 529 plans are reported as part of parental investments.

You will find on the CSS Profile form:

1. Student assets are assessed at 25% per year.
2. Does provide allowance for unreimbursed medical and dental expenses over 3.5% AGI (excluded on the FAFSA)
3. Adds back losses from the 1040, which can increase the EFC
4. Can factor in an allowance from elementary and/or secondary school tuition for siblings
5. Does assess your home equity
6. Does assess business assets
7. Student-owned 529 plans are considered a student asset.

The FAFSA form and the Federal Methodology help a college to determine your expected family contribution and your financial need. Colleges use this information to help them know if a family is qualified to receive any federal financial aid.

However, the financial aid officer (FAO) and/or enrollment manager (EM) at each individual college have the ability to increase your EFC or lower your EFC number to determine a family's "ability to pay." The FAO and EM have a great deal of latitude in determining which students should receive the college's own institutional aid such as tuition discounts, grants, and scholarships. The colleges have the ability to asses a family's "ability to pay" differently than the Department of Education EFC number because the colleges can use the EFC generated by the FAFSA form or the EFC number on the College Board CSS Profile form.

Let me give you a good case study. My client is a single mother with two daughters in high school. The mother works as a nurse at a local hospital, and the oldest daughter is a senior in high school and is getting recruited to play basketball at a few Division III colleges. We helped the daughter narrow down her college choices earlier in the year, and now I am in the final stages of helping this family make the decision on where the daughter will attend college. The cost of college is a large factor in the decision of where she might attend college.

The daughter has narrowed down her college choices between two private colleges that she likes, and both colleges have given the family an initial financial aid offer. Unfortunately, the two colleges did not meet her entire financial need as determined by the need-based financial aid calculation on the initial award letters. Both colleges have left a financial "gap" that the mother cannot afford.

A few weeks ago, I helped the family write a financial aid appeal letter to the financial aid office because the mother's income for this year is down by more than 30% due to the hospital dramatically reducing her overtime hours. I received the following e-mail from her today:

> *This is an award letter we received from the FAO this weekend. I also wanted to ask if you might know who could have updated the FAFSA form? I got an e-mail yesterday that said it had been updated, but I have not updated it!!!*
> *Thanks,*
> *Susan*

I asked Susan to forward me the e-mail that she received so I could take a look at it. Below is the e-mail from one of the college's director of admissions:

> *Dear Susan - I have bad news and good news for you... I'm starting with the bad news. The updated award is still not significantly better than our first offer, even with a $1,500 basketball scholarship.*
>
> *Your award from the other college is $29,356 - $13,850 scholarship/grant assistance = $15,506 after scholarship/grant assistance.*
>
> *Our financial offer is $33,219 - $17,450 scholarship/grant assistance = $15,769 after scholarship/grant assistance.*
>
> *That's just a $263 dollar differential. So that's the bad news.*

*Now the good news. Our financial aid director DID review your special circumstances request again, and **she made some changes to Ashley's FAFSA.** Your daughter will now be receiving an additional $4,000 per year through the federal Pell Grant program! Here is her updated award, which should arrive in the mail soon.*

Fund	Amount	Status	Created Date
Merit Scholarship	$6,000.00	Pending	02/25/2010
Founders Grant	$4,600.00	Pending	02/25/2010
NCLTG	$1,850.00	Pending	02/25/2010
NCCG	$3,000.00	Pending	02/25/2010
Work-study	$1,600.00	Pending	02/25/2010
Direct Loan (subsidized)	$3,500.00	Pending	02/25/2010
Direct Loan (unsubsidized)	$2,000.00	Pending	02/25/2010
Pastor's Certificate	$1,000.00	Pending	04/07/2010
Greatest Gift	$1,000.00	Pending	04/07/2010
Pell Grant	$4,000.00	Pending	05/21/2010
Totals:	$28,550.00		

Our total cost is approximately $33,200 and everything except the work-study can be subtracted from the total, leaving a balance of approximately $6,250 for the year after scholarships, grants, and loans.

The balance can be paid with a Direct Parent PLUS Loan, one of our payment plans, or you can take out an alternative student loan (which is not preferred unless necessary).

Call me if you have questions/concerns!
– Casey
Director of Admissions

After reviewing the e-mail, I knew exactly what had happened. I informed her that colleges have the authority to make corrections at their discretion. The college made the correction based on her special circumstance letter that we helped her write a few weeks ago. In this case, the corrections made by the financial aid officer (FAO) were a good thing because it lowered the family's EFC enough to qualify this family for the Pell Grant! I hope you are asking the question, "Why did the college FAO not offer her the Pell Grant to begin with?"

Below is the e-mail she received from the Department of Education concerning the correction to her EFC calculation:

Sent: Tuesday, May 25, 2010 7:57 AM
Subject: Corrected FAFSA Results - 2010-2011 Student Aid Report

Your Correction to your Free Application for Federal Student Aid (FAFSA) has been processed and the data will be made available to the school(s) listed on your corrected FAFSA. The financial aid office at your school will contact you if additional information is required.

The Financial Aid Administrator (FAA) at your school has made corrections to your application. If you think you need to make additional corrections, please contact your FAA before doing so…

Thank You,

U.S. Department of Education
Federal Student Aid

As you can see, the financial aid officer and/or enrollment manager at this college had the ability to increase EFC or lower the EFC number to determine a family's "ability to pay." The FAO and EM have a great deal of latitude in determining which student should receive any financial aid.

You may be asking yourself why it is important to know the difference between EFC and "ability to pay." Unlike the case study I just mentioned, most middle-class Americans do not qualify for need-based aid unless their student attends a very pricey private college.

If you want to reduce the cost of college and you don't qualify for need-based aid, I will show you strategies that you can use to reduce your "ability to pay" and get as much aid as possible in the coming chapters.

CHAPTER 12

Mistake #11: Spending Too Much Time and Money to Find Private Scholarships

The majority of American families believe the only way to reduce the cost of college is to get private scholarships. I encourage my families to try to get as many private or "outside" scholarships as they can. There are thousands and maybe even millions of dollars in private scholarships available for families if they are diligent.

Private scholarships can be awarded nationally, such as the Coca-Cola Scholarships and the AXA Achievement Scholarship. Most families will find success looking locally, then statewide, and finally nationally for private scholarships. For example, families should start at:

1. Local civic organizations (Lions Club, Kiwanis Club, Rotary Club, etc.)
2. Workplace scholarships (Duke Scholarship, McDonald's, Baskin-Robbins, etc.)
3. Local church, synagogue, mosque, etc.

The National Postsecondary Student Aid Study (NPSAS) is a large survey conducted every three to four years by the National Center for Education Statistics (NCES) to gather information on how students pay for college. The survey is so large that it represents quite a large sample of the overall student population. NPSAS's survey contains information about private sector or outside scholarships by not including any government, employer, and institutional aid, such as athletic scholarships. The following tables provide statistics for students based on private sector aid.

(You can read more about this at www.finaid.org/scholarships/award count.phtml.)

NPSAS Undergraduate Students				
Study Year	Average Scholarship Amount	Percentage Receiving Scholarships	Number of Recipients	Amount of Awards
1989-1990	$1,320.70	3.20%	526,000	$695 million
1992-1993	$1,440.52	3.50%	638,974	$920 million
1995-1996	$1,560.91	3.50%	577,000	$900 million
1999-2000	$2,050.84	6.90%	1,141,000	$2.34 billion
2003-2004	$1,982.02	6.70%	1,276,000	$2.53 billion
2007-2008	$2,523.31	5.50%	1,152,300	$2.91 billion

Unfortunately, only around 5.5% of all students in 2007-2008 in America receive private scholarships. Moreover, these scholarships are usually *only awarded for one year* for an average of $2,523.31.

Most importantly, these private scholarships can reduce your financial aid package dollar for dollar! It is a federal mandate that colleges consider any private scholarships when considering your financial aid package. For example, let's consider a family with an EFC of $10,000 a year going to a college with a cost of attendance (COA) of $25,000 a year. The need-based aid calculation would look like:

$$
\begin{array}{lr}
\text{COA:} & \$25,000 \\
\text{-EFC:} & \$10,000 \\
\hline
\text{Financial Need:} & \$15,000 \\
\end{array}
$$

If this student receives a $5,000 dollar scholarship from the mother's employer, the financial aid officer could reduce the financial need to only $10,000:

$$
\begin{array}{lr}
\text{COA:} & \$25,000 \\
\text{-EFC:} & \$10,000 \\
\hline
\text{Financial Need:} & \$15,000 \\
\text{Private Scholarship:} & (\$5,000) \\
\text{New Financial Need:} & \$10,000 \\
\end{array}
$$

I do encourage you to look for private scholarships, but certainly don't spend too much time looking and never pay anyone or any company to search for private scholarships. I have included a number of free scholarship resources at the end of this book to help you with this endeavor.

Not only is it easier to qualify for merit awards and tuitions discounts, but there is much more of it! The tuition discounts and merit aid is what I consider to be the low-hanging fruit.

CHAPTER 13

Knowing the Rules of the Game

"I don't think much of a man who is not wiser today than he was yesterday."
— Abraham Lincoln

It is not in the best interest of the college or the financial aid officer (FAO) for you to know the rules of the game. They want you to be confused about the financial aid process, and they want to control the information that the general public, students, parents, and the guidance counselors know about financial aid. Why do you think that they volunteer to speak at your local high school's college night?

I have a five-year-old son who I was teaching the game of Connect Four. He had the red-colored checkers and I had the yellow. When we first started to play the game, I showed him if I was able to get four yellow checkers in a row, I would win the game. As you can imagine, I won the first few games until he got a better understanding of the strategies and the rules of the game. Once he understood the rules and the strategies, he was able to win or at least tie.

Like my son when he was first introduced to Connect Four, most parents are playing the game of college planning thinking they know the rules and the strategies of the game. They believe that they have been taught these rules and strategies by the colleges, by the media, and by the counselors at the local high school. Unfortunately, the old rules that applied when most of the mothers and fathers went off to college no longer work in the game of college planning. That is why you will sometimes see high school valedictorians not receive much financial aid or merit aid today when 20 years ago they were almost guaranteed great college financial awards. The strategies colleges use to play the game have dramatically changed, and families need to know that. If you do not change how you play, you will always lose the game.

Let me give you an example: The Moore family came into my office through a referral from the Richards family. They knew that I was able to save the Richards family thousands of dollars in college costs, and they wanted me to help them with college costs for their next child, who was a junior in high school. The Moores' oldest son was a senior in college at Washington and Lee University in Virginia and did not receive any financial assistance from Washington and Lee.

The Moores knew that their son had great grades in high school and good SAT scores. He graduated as the valedictorian of his class and scored in the 95th percentile on his SAT. Their son was also very involved with church and had many hours of community service. They were under the false assumption that he would get a lot of merit aid, grants, and scholarships from the college. The only aid that they received from the university was the Unsubsidized Stafford Loan, worth approximately $5,500 from the college that cost approximately $56,000 at the time of attendance.

Like most families today, they believed the college rules of 20 or 30 years ago still apply. They believed that if your child makes good grades, has a good standardized test scores, and has good extracurricular activities, your child will receive scholarships and money from the colleges and universities.

The Moore family did everything right to position their son for success in the game of college planning by encouraging their son to get great grades and a high GPA, to take hard classes in high school, to have wonderful extracurricular activities, and to study hard for the SAT test. However, they failed to realize that colleges now are using sophisticated data mining and computer modeling to help them decide which families will receive aid and which ones will not. They failed to understand that colleges are businesses, and as businesses they will not give out their money if they do not have to do so. The FAOs, enrollment managers, and presidents of the colleges are just like you and I when it comes to money. You are not going to give away your cash if you do not have to, and neither does a college.

Like the Moore family, some of my clients are parents with one child in college who received very little financial assistance from the college. They now understand that the strategies have changed. They failed to realize that the colleges and universities are playing the game differently, and they now know that they need help to understand the new rules. These parents are usually paying the full cost of college, and they made the bad assumption that they were going to receive aid because they had a good student. They do not want to make the same mistake twice.

Rules of the Game

Before I can show you how to win the game, I need to explain the rules of the game. I was watching the Quail Hallow Golf Tournament in Charlotte, NC, recently, and I was amazed by how much better the professional golfers are than the average golfer. The majority of the professional golfers can strike the golf ball further, have more control, and are much better at chipping and putting than you or I. All the professional golfers also have the best equipment in the world, which makes them that much better. You and I can purchase the same equipment that the professional golfers use, but that does not mean we will be as good as they are. In my case, I just hit the ball further in the woods when I purchase a new driver. Having the best equipment is important, but having the skill and the knowledge of a professional golfer is much more important to being a better golfer. That is why so many people pay for a golf coach or teacher to help them improve their game.

I want to be your college coach, and I am going to teach you the fundamentals of the college game. We are going to spend the next few chapters teaching you the basics and the fundamentals of college financial aid. This will be the equivalent of a golfer practicing his or her swing on a golf range. Once you feel comfortable with your swing, or the basics of college planning, we will then move on to the right clubs—the specific strategies to use to reduce the cost of college.

Rule One: Understand the Different Types of Financial Aid

There are two basic forms of financial aid: need-based aid and merit-based aid. Let's start with merit-based aid. Merit aid is basically financial assistance based upon the talent of the student. Merit aid is sometimes referred to as tuition discounts. This talent could be anything from a basketball scholarship, money to sing in the college choir, or aid based upon high SAT scores. This is financial aid that is not supposed to be dependent on a family's finances but rather on the student's academic, artistic, or athletic ability.

Not all colleges give merit aid. In general, the more selective the college, the less likely they are to give merit-based aid. The good news is that institutional merit aid increased by 212% from 1995 to 2004.

Let's begin to look at how a college determines who receives merit aid. For example, let's envision you were working for a college and you were on the committee to decide which college applicant would receive the college's $20,000 Merit Scholarship. You have narrowed down and eliminated all potential applicants to two remaining students. Both students have great GPAs and high school transcripts. Both students have scored about the same on the SAT. What do you think you would look at next to help separate the two applicants? If you said extracurricular activities (ECs), you would be right. Most colleges use extracurricular activities to help separate the candidates if all other variables are about the same.

As you can see, ECs are extremely important. When I was in high school, I tried to join every club and organization to build my college transcript or college resume. Today, most colleges are not looking for someone who just joined a lot of different clubs. Most colleges are looking for students who are dedicated to a cause and make a difference while in the club or organization. For example, a student should not join the Spanish club, DECA club, FCA club, Key club, etc. just to make himself or herself look good because he or she is a member of a number of different clubs. Instead, the student should join a few clubs that really interest him or her and stay involved in those clubs for multiple years. While in the club, the student should try to make a difference by being involved with the activities or showing leadership through volunteering or becoming an officer in the club or organization. The student could head a committee, become the president of the club, or be the leader of an activity that made a difference at the school or in the community.

Extracurricular activities are not just clubs. It could also mean being involved in sports, church youth groups, work, etc. As long as a student is showing dedication to a cause and making a difference, the colleges will be impressed.

ECs are very important, especially for merit aid awards, to separate yourself from the competition. Colleges are supposed to look at a student's grades, test scores, hobbies, special talents, and extracurricular activities to determine if a student receives merit aid. Sometimes this is not the only thing they look at to determine merit aid awards. Can a parent's income and assets come into play for merit aid scholarships? In some cases, your income and assets do play a role in merit aid.

Most colleges will not tell you this or admit to this because it is politically incorrect to mention that your income and assets play a role in merit aid decisions. After all, isn't merit aid supposed to be based on the talent of the student?

You probably don't believe me because your guidance counselor has not told you this and the college representative did not tell you this. Let me give you a few examples from some merit aid applications.

Below is the exact wording of a merit aid application from one of the state universities in North Carolina:

Essay Question

1. What are your major accomplishments and why to you consider them significant?

2. Who, of everyone living and dead, would you like to meet and why?

3. When you look back on your life in thirty years, what would it take for you to consider your life successful?

Checklist for a Complete Scholarship Application:

___ Application Attached

___ Completed Free Application for Federal Student Aid

___ Accepted by the College

___ Essay

Why would a college need you to complete the FASFA if this merit scholarship is based entirely on the merit of the child and not the family's income and assets?

This is another great example. Below is the exact wording of an acceptance letter a student of mine received from Gardner-Webb University:

"We have designed our Great Choice Program, which consist of 150 scholarships, to be awarded on a first come, first serve basis, to eligible students. We encourage you to accept our offer of admissions and to return the enclosed Great Choice Student Aid Profile form. Upon receiving this we will put together an early estimate financial aid package. This package will allow you to have a clear picture as it relates to cost of attendance, in addition the sooner you respond, the better chance you have at receiving one of our select Great Choice Scholarships."

In order to receive one of the 150 scholarships at this university, the family must complete the "Great Choice Student Aid Profile form" in which the family's income and assets will need to be listed. Why would Gardner-Webb need a family to complete their Great Choice Student Aid form before the college makes a decision on merit scholarship money?

The next example is taken from Campbell University's Web site in which it lists its academic scholarship information. On its Web site, you will see five columns:

Scholarship	Qualifications	Commitment	Amount	Procedure
Presidential	GPA: 3.4-4.0	4 yrs, Min GPA	$14,000	Apply to University
	SAT: 1725 +			*Complete FAFSA

As you can see, you need to apply to the university and complete the FAFSA. Again, why would this family need to complete the FAFSA form unless a family's income and assets play a role in this decision?

The final example is from the Texas Common Application for its freshman **scholarship application**. *It is required to be completed.* Below are a few of the questions on the required scholarship application:

Funds for college saved by you: $_____

Funds for college saved by others: $_____

Projected parental support (annual): $_____

Your total annual income: $_____

Your spouse's total annual income: $_____

Biological Father's Information

1. Occupation:

2. Employer:

3. Total Annual Income: $_____

Biological Mother's Information:

1. Occupation:

2. Employer:

3. Total Annual Income: $_____

Why would a parent need to supply this information if the scholarship is based only on the talent or merit of the student?

The second type of financial aid is called **need-based aid**. The basic formula for calculating need-based aid has not changed in almost 30 years:

1. Cost of Attendance (COA)

2. Expected Family Contribution (EFC)

3. Need-based Aid / Financial Need (FN)

The college's cost of attendance (COA) minus the expected family contribution (EFC) equals the student's financial need (FN), which is the maximum need-based aid that a family can receive. Need analysis is the process in which the government and the colleges determine your financial need.

The COA is the total cost for the student to attend a college. This would include tuition, room and board, fees, books and supplies, transportation, and personal and incidental expenses. Schools define COA differently, so make sure you know how they define the COA if you are trying to determine your need-based aid.

The EFC is the minimum amount of money the family is expected to pay toward the student's education. This number is calculated on your behalf by the government and the colleges.

Isn't it nice that the government and the colleges will tell you how much they think you can afford to pay? The EFC is calculated by the Federal Methodology and the Institutional Methodology.

Rule Two: Get Familiar with the Different Financial Aid Forms and Complete Them Early

Some colleges use the Federal Methodology (FM) to determine your EFC number, or how much they think you can afford to pay. Most all public colleges use the FM. All four-year colleges that give out federal need-based aid use the FM and the FAFSA to arrive at this number. The FAFSA form will look at your family size, age of the older parent, parent and student's assets, parent and student's taxable and nontaxable income, taxes paid, and the student's dependency status. The FM does not consider the net value of your home, but it will consider second homes or other real estate values.

To calculate your EFC using the FM, you can go www.FSFSA4 caster.ed.gov. The government uses the FM to determine if you are eligible to receive federal money such as the Pell Grant, SEOGs, and the Stafford Loans.

A lot of the financial aid that the colleges give is on a first-come, first-served basis, so don't wait until your taxes are complete in April to start this form. I would suggest you complete the form during the first few weeks in January of a student's senior year in high school. January 1st of the student's senior year in high school is the earliest you can complete the FAFSA form. If you do your own taxes, please complete them as early as possible. If you use a CPA, please let them know that you need your taxes completed ASAP for financial aid purposes. You might also want to complete the FAFSA form using estimated numbers based on your last year's tax return. Once your tax return is complete, you can then log into your FAFSA form and update the numbers using your current tax return. By doing it this way, you can make sure your family is not left out and you maximize your family's chances of getting as much aid as possible.

Some private colleges and a few public colleges use the Institutional Method (IM) to determine your EFC. A college that uses the IM will require you to complete the Financial Aid Profile (FAP) in addition to the FASFA form to determine your EFC. Also known as the CSS Profile form, the FAP looks at family size, age of the older parent, parent and student's assets, parent and student's taxable and nontaxable income, taxes paid, home equity, and the student's dependency. The CSS Profile form is more complicated and more detailed than the FASFA form. The numbers on the FASFA and the FAP form need to correspond or the colleges will reject the forms.

Both the CSS Profile form and the FAFSA form do not take into consideration any unsecured consumer debt!

A few colleges require the CSS Profile form to be completed as *early as November*! So make sure you pay attention to the due dates of the colleges you wish to apply to.

Rule Three: Understand Enrollment Management

This is the most important rule to know! If you understand enrollment management (EM), then you will succeed in the college game. Almost all colleges and universities in the United States and Canada follow the rules of EM. EM has changed the college game, and it is because of EM that the college rules of 20 years ago no longer apply and we all must adapt.

Enrollment management (EM) is the calculated and selective use of offers of financial aid to help shape the makeup of an incoming freshman class. Institutions offer this aid to specific students to help achieve the college's goals. *This unique aid is not based upon the students' need or academic merit.*

Colleges often use EM as a way to compete with other rival institutions and further the goals of the each individual school. EM implements strategies derived from sophisticated use of data mining and computer simulations to predict the outcome that various financial aid offers will have on the incoming freshman class. Some of the questions that EM professionals try to answer with computer modeling and data mining include:

1. Can I increase "net tuition revenue" streams?

2. Can I increase the proportion of entering students capable of paying all or most of the cost of attendance?

3. Can I "admit-deny"? (Admit-deny means discouraging enrollment of low-income students by offering inadequate financial assistance, knowing that they will not attend. At the same time, the institutions publicly state that they are admitting and offering aid to this specific group of families.)

4. Can I increase diversity?

Many colleges and universities have combined former admissions and financial aid departments into one enrollment management office. In the large universities, you could have 40 individuals working in the EM office. Enrollment managers are individuals who oversee the entire admissions and financial aid process to increase retention, net revenue streams, geographic goals, and ethnic diversity at the schools. There are also outside consulting firms that play a big part in helping colleges make these decisions:

1. Noel Levitz
2. Scannell and Kurz
3. Art and Science

4. Blackbaud
5. Maguire Associates
6. American Association of Collegiate Registrars & Admissions Officers (AACRAO)
7. Lawlor Group

These consulting firms never tell a college specifically what to do with a particular student or family, but they do present the colleges options to consider. For example, they might demonstrate how a family will react to various financial aid packages. The consulting firms will show the colleges and universities the different types of freshman classes who could enroll in their school if the school adopts and implements specific techniques laid out by the firms. For example, a college could choose between a menu of options that would: maximize net tuition revenue, increase net SAT scores across the entire class, increase diversity, or even increase a specific major at a college (like nursing). Of course, there are trade-offs among the different strategies. With one incoming class, a school might be able to increase academic quality, but net tuition revenue and diversity will probably decline.

Recruiting Funnel

Enrollment managers grade and qualify student prospects at all the various stages of the "recruiting funnel" so they can manage resources better by directing them toward students who will more likely enroll.

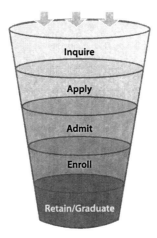

To increase the number of prospects, some colleges are buying tens of thousands of prospective student name lists and mailing expensive marketing pieces to increase interest in the school. I read that some private colleges spend approximately $1,960 on recruiting per student and public colleges spend $516 per student.

These colleges know that there are students who *will not* enroll no matter what a college does and some students *who will* enroll no matter what the college does not do. The majority of students lies between these two extremes, and the EMs grade them based on their desirability for the school and interest in actually coming to the school.

The EMs believe that by grading and classifying the prospective students into groups, marketing efforts and resources can be individualized among the various groups to get better recruiting results by focusing on the prospective students who are most likely to enroll. The colleges would like to get their message to the right potential students at the right time, and the computer modeling allows them to achieve this. The institutions believe that this will save marketing costs on postage, printing, travel, and phone calls. They also believe that this saves the college valuable time and effort from the admissions and financial aid staff.

EMs also believe that their services help focus resources on the school's most attractive potential students. The institution will grade the desirability of the student at the prospect, inquiry, applicant, and admit stages. During these stages, the college or university will determine what type of student it wishes to enroll and what type of student would help the school achieve its goals. The institution will identify and eliminate those students with little or no interest and target the students whom the institution would like to recruit. Colleges use this system to focus on the approximately 20% of the applicant pool that will make up the majority of the freshman class.

The outside consulting firms help the institutions and EMs to customize the grading and how each college will qualify prospective students. These outside consulting firms offer admissions office software and enrollment management programs that calculate advanced statistical methods to assist these colleges and universities to grade and qualify each student.

Once the consulting firms and the institutions customize and develop these models, all prospective students are scored based upon their likelihood to enroll. The higher the potential student scores, the better match he or she is for the institution.

Prospect	Score out of 1,000	Classification
Jeff Jones	847	High Priority: Likely to enroll
Jason Bass	615	Medium Priority: Can be in influenced
Bryan Smith	397	Low Priority: Unlikely to enroll

Many colleges and universities believe that without a way to predict behavior, all three of the above students would receive the same amount of marketing attention and valuable resources. These institutions believe that this modeling helps them not waste these resources on the students who would probably not enroll. Many of these same institutions separate their lead pool of students into five buckets so that they can focus on the top 20% of the pool and ignore the bottom 20%.

Abilene Christian University's prospective student pool had grown so large in recent years that it was draining the university's budget and becoming difficult for the university to manage. In 2000, the university started using enrollment management to increase diversity, enroll better students, and focus on students from a certain religious denomination. Since implementing enrollment management, the university has increased their applications by more than 25.1%, and their total enrollment also increased by 10.5% with between 22% and 40% more applications from the targeted recruiting segments than the previous two years. Moreover, the school was able to get a better mix of students in its application pool. The predictive modeling showed the school how to leverage their resources and reduce costs while increasing the amount and frequency of their mailings to the students in their lead pool who were most likely to enroll.

Data Mining

Data mining is essential for accurate modeling for enrollment management. Below are some of the data that the colleges frequently collect about the prospective students and their families:

1. How many times the student has made contact with the school
2. The time between the student-initiated contacts
3. First contact source
4. Campus visits
5. Household data from national consumer databases
6. ACT/SAT scores and questions answered when registering for the test
7. College fair attendance
8. Geographic market area
9. Geodemographic code
10. Submission of early aid estimator
11. Student academic profile

Let's look at a few of the above items that colleges use to collect information about a prospective student and family. What can "geodemographic code" tell a college or university about a certain family? Well, a geodemographic code is able to give socio-demographic features of a certain area. Using these codes, the institutions can gain information such as average household income, net worth, education attainment by family members, and other socio-demographic attributes of certain areas throughout the United States.

Descriptor and Recruitment Plus are two of the geodemographic computer programs that colleges and universities use to identify and tag groups of students according to neighborhoods in which a student lives and high schools that they attend. By using these programs, a college can target for recruitment specific students who meet academic, geographic, and financial profiles that the college wants to attract.

The institutions also obtain information from the ACT and SAT as early as a student's sophomore year in high school. When a family signs up to take the ACT or SAT, you are asked a variety of questions such as:

1. What is your ethnicity?
2. How many hours do you spend in community service?
3. What major are you interested in?
4. In what area of the country are you going to want to live?
5. **What are your top four college picks in numerical order?**
6. **Do you intend to apply for need-based aid?**

The College Board, the ACT, and the National Research Center for College and University Admissions sell this information to the colleges and universities. The schools use this information to know who their competitors are and their market position.

The article "Colleges Turn to Consultants to Shape the Freshman Class," first published in T*he Chronicle of Higher Education*, tells a story about Baylor University, Noel-Levitz, and a prospective student named Chris Kouba. Noel-Levitz designed an EM model for Baylor to show the school the likelihood that a potential student would enroll in their college based upon characteristics of students who enrolled in the past.

Mr. Kouba was a senior in high school at the time, had scored 1180 (out 1600) on the SAT, and had a GPA near the top of his class. Noel-Levitz recognized that Mr. Kouba was the type of student that Baylor would like to recruit and identified him as a great prospect by giving Mr. Kouba a score near the top of Baylor's chart of freshman prospects.

You might be wondering what information Baylor knew about Mr. Kouba to make him such a hot commodity and to help them predict he would enroll in the college. Listed below is what helped Noel-Levitz and Baylor rate him so high using their computer models.

1. Three campus visits
2. Interest in becoming a minister
3. *Parents' residence* in a middle-class suburb that often sends students to Baylor

4. *Credit history of the parents* obtained from TransUnion (credit tracking)

5. *Estimated income of family*

Once Baylor identified the student and family as a top priority, the school inundated the student with mail and other marketing pieces arriving almost once a week. Chris Kouba ultimately did decide to attend Baylor University.

Colleges and universities are using enrollment management to shape their freshman classes so they can increase revenue, increase the number of students who can pay the full tuition, decrease the proportion of poor students by offering inadequate offers with "admit-deny" practices, and increase ethnic diversity. They are able to accomplish this by using data mining and sophisticated computer modeling to predict which students to recruit and what type of aid to offer.

Tuition Discounting

Tuition discounting or financial aid leveraging is the most controversial enrollment management practice. Some think that tuition discounting is a way for the colleges and universities to manipulate their prices for the benefit of the college and not for the well-being of the students. *Colleges and universities are now using need-based aid, institutional grants, merit aid, and tuition discounts to increase the proportion of targeted students who will attend their respective schools.*

Enrollment management and tuition discounting have changed the rules of the college game dramatically since the early 1990s. Enrollment management was introduced in the 1970s, but it really took hold in the early 1990s.

Also, remember that the financial aid officer (FAO) and/or enrollment manager (EM) at a college has the ability to increase or lower the EFC to determine a family's ability to pay. The FAO and EM have a great deal of latitude in determining which student should receive any financial aid. They collect as much data as they can on the student and the family by data mining. They use this information and very sophisticated computer software to help them make decisions on the type of student the school wants to recruit. The college or university will then use mathematic algorithms and computer modeling to help the college or university determine if they would like to offer the student any need-based aid, merit-based aid, grants, or tuition discounts.

Knowing the rules of the game is the first step to playing the college funding game the right way. Understanding these rules is essential to getting great financial aid award letters:

1. **Rule One: Understand the Different Types Financial Aid**
2. **Rule Two: Get Familiar with the Different Financial Aid Forms and Complete Them Early**
3. **Rule Three: Understand Enrollment Management**

CHAPTER 14

STEP 1: The Commitment

"Many people think amateurs do not play for money, but they play for the love of the game. In reality, the reason amateurs are amateurs are because they do not love the game enough."
– Stephen Pressfield

Now that we've covered the biggest blunders a family can make and laid the groundwork of knowing the rules of the college funding game, I can show you how to actually play the game. But before we begin the steps for how to save you thousands of dollars in college costs, there's a commitment I will ask each of you to make. This will ensure that you will make the most of the strategies that I will share in the following chapters and assist you with implementing and putting these strategies into action.

No matter what your student's current high school transcript might look like or where your family is financially, the first step for paying wholesale, not retail, for your child's college is to have commitment, faith, and desire. You need to have the faith that if you follow my steps, you will succeed. Because you have read this far in my book, it proves you have the desire to win this college funding game. Finally, you must be committed to follow through to complete each step.

With your desire, commitment, and the willingness to have faith in my proven system of reducing college costs, you will achieve success.

But if you are not committed and you only follow a few of the steps, you will probably be like most middle-class families in America that pay the retail price for college.

My proven systems works without fail (if the simple steps are followed). My system does not list every detailed step a student or parent must take because the book would be too large for print. These are the most significant steps a family must take to achieve the desired return.

I need from you the desire and the faith to follow the simple steps I present to you in this book.

Now choose to be one of the few middle-class Americans who save hundreds of thousands of dollars in college costs. Join my other satisfied clients by signing on the next page:

College Aid for Middle Class America
Commitment for Parents

I have a smart, gifted child. I will encourage, listen to, and help my child through this stressful time. I will help facilitate college visits, and I will help keep track of all the application and financial aid deadlines. I will listen to the opinions of other parents, but I will let my child make up his or her own opinion about his or her college choices. I know my child's self-worth does not revolve around the college that he or she attends. I recognize that, as a parent, my first instinct is to keep my child close to home to help protect him or her from making mistakes. I promise to control this "nesting" instinct and not to allow my anxiety over my child moving into young adulthood to limit my child's college search if he or she so desires to move away. I will only make educated suggestions to my child and not dictate the college search or selection. I know this will be a very stressful time for me and especially for my child, but I will try to lessen the stress by being proactive, but not pushy.

I will face the financial reality of helping pay for my child's college education and not allow him or her to take this burden solely on his or her shoulders. I will speak honestly to my child about how the cost of college will help determine the final college selection. I will follow the steps to ensure we find a variety of schools that are suitable for my child and are affordable for me. I will use my calculator as well as my heart when we make the final college selection.

Signed this_____day of_____20____.

_____
Your Signature

As further confirmation of your commitment, please go to
www.college aidformiddleclass.com. It's free, and I will e-mail
you a certificate of commitment celebrating your critical first step.

CHAPTER 15

STEP 2: Take Action

"Education is what remains after one has forgotten everything he learned in school."
– Albert Einstein

Thank you for taking the first step to becoming one of the enlightened families in America. You are well on your way to joining the others who have greatly reduced the cost of college for their children.

The second critical component of the magnificent power of commitment is **action and progress.** Our lives are often so busy that it is easy to get distracted and put things off, but when we are committed to something, we are more likely to take action toward it every day. You are committed to providing food and shelter for your family, so you take the action to go to work every day to earn a paycheck to provide for your family. Without the commitment or the desire to support your family, you probably would not go to work every day.

We all want to see immediate results, but that is not how long-term success is achieved. Success is a process that must be followed, and you must take action! I will show you simple, easy disciplines that, if followed, will achieve the results you want. You might be asking yourself, "Why don't all families achieve these results?" Because every action that seems easy to do is not always easy to do. It is easy to read how to do something, but it's often hard to take action and follow the process.

I heard a good quote once: "You will not find too many millionaires that bowl over a 100." I took this to mean that the millionaires gave up bowling leagues to spend time elsewhere to make their fortunes. The small amount of time and money that you invested to purchase and read my book will be worthless unless you take action. Moreover, the small amount of time it takes to complete these steps will save you thousands of dollars in college costs.

In my business, I coach families on how to achieve a college degree for less than they thought was possible by providing them with very simple, easy-to-follow steps. I found that it's far easier to complete steps one at a time rather than trying to complete multiple tasks at the same time or combining steps because you believe it will save time and energy.

For example, some parents might believe that they can skip step 1 through step 4. These families believe it is okay to go directly to step 5, narrowing down their college selection for the student. While they will have the results faster initially, it usually backfires in the end when it comes time to make the final college selection.

For example, a child might be emotionally attached to a very expensive college. The college did not offer the family any financial aid, but the child insists on attending and pressures the parents to let him or her go to this college even though it may mean financial ruin for the family. Why? Because steps 1 through 4 were neglected and the parents did not set any standards or goals for the student. The parents never spoke honestly about the financial realities that most parents face when it comes to paying for college.

If you have not yet done so, go to **www.collegeaidformiddleclass.com** and sign up. By sharing your commitment with us, you are taking an important first step by taking action! This will dramatically improve your probability of achieving college funding success.

As a College Aid for Middle Class America Member, you are eligible for free Web site training and free tools to help you step by step. You will find a series of tools and exercises to support you as you go through the steps. In addition, as part of your free membership, you will receive a series of College Aid for Middle Class America e-mails. Each e-mail is designed to inform, inspire, and educate you through this process.

Is College an Asset or Liability?

Do you want a college degree to be an asset or a liability? An asset is anything that puts money in your pocket and a liability is anything that takes money out of your pocket. Is getting a college degree an asset or a liability?

To determine if college is an asset or not, you have to look at the actual financial numbers!

For instance, if you purchased a stock for $100, most people would consider the stock an asset. If you were able to sell the stock for $200, it would be an asset because you sold it for more than you purchased. But if you sold the stock for $10, it would be considered a liability because you sold it for less than you purchased it.

Most families would consider college an asset. I agree that a college degree can become a very prosperous asset with an infinite rate of return. However, a college degree can also easily become a huge liability for a family. When I spent some time in Texas, I learned the phrase, "big hat, no cattle." In Texas, this means that someone who lives in a big house and drives an expensive car has no money. Many families in America also treat a college degree in the same fashion.

Some families in America send their children off to well-known, very expensive colleges. They are initially very proud and brag to others about the prestigious colleges their children attend. They believe that since these colleges have such a great reputation and are ranked high in all the college periodicals, surely their children will receive a fine education and get high-paying jobs when they graduate.

They are also hoping that the school's name on the diploma will somehow magically pay for this very high cost of education sometime in the future because they cannot afford the college bill! Each family is forced to take out thousands of dollars in loans every year with high interest rates that will burden them for the rest of their lives. The parents know that both they and the child will be paying back loans for many years. They are rolling the dice and hoping this large gamble pays off. As they say in Texas, this family has a big hat and no cattle. I like to say this family is looking good but going nowhere. This college degree will more than likely become a liability for the rest of their lives!

Wealth is measured in time, not in money. For example, if a family has $100,000 in savings and their monthly expenses are $10,000, then their wealth is 10 months. By choosing an expensive college, a family is wagering not only their financial future, but the extra amount of time that a family or the student will need to work to pay off this expensive college. They are dramatically reducing their current and future wealth. Following my simple steps will help reduce the cost of college and reduce the time you will need to pay off any college costs. I will show you how to make sure a college degree becomes an asset!

When I first moved to Charlotte, I lived beside a retired married couple. They were always dressed well, and their yard was always green and manicured. One day when I saw the elderly man out in the yard, I took the opportunity to introduce myself to my new neighbor. After a few minutes of getting to know him, I asked him what he did for a living when he was working full time. He told me he was a proselyte. I had heard this term once before in religious circles, so I asked him if he was a priest, rabbi, or religious leader before he retired. He got a good chuckle from my question and told me, "No, I was not a priest, a rabbi, nor did I work for any church or religion."

He explained that the term "proselyte" is used to describe a person who has changed from one opinion or religious belief to another. "I helped people change from one company to another," he said. "Some people called me a headhunter, but I always preferred the term 'proselyte.'" He then went on to tell me about the hundreds of men and women he recruited from just a few companies over the years. He specialized in recruiting and helping hire only the uppermost management, vice presidents, and CEOs. Since I was just a few years out of college at the time, I wanted to know what made these individuals stand out from the crowd and what qualifications he looked for when reviewing the candidates.

His answer surprised me and changed my entire outlook on my career. He said, "The most important quality or skill I looked for is job performance. We already knew about the individual before we recruited him. We would do our homework on him to make sure he was what we were looking for in a high management position. The individuals that we recruited would always be great employees and would have a history of outstanding job performance with their current employer. We knew all of this before we even began the process to 'proselyte' them."

I thought he might be just giving me the company line and the politically correct answer of just hiring the best worker, so I then asked if he only recruited people who graduated from certain prominent or well-known colleges. He said, "Honestly, I might glance at the college to make sure they received a degree from college, but the specifics of the degree I did not care about, nor did I care about the where they attended college. Really, the most important factor is outstanding prior job performance at their current job!"

My illusion of the grandeur of a college name suddenly faded!

I like to think of a business like an NFL team during draft day. Every NFL team spends millions of dollars each year evaluating talent by looking at hours of tape, speaking to college coaches, sending scouts to watch college games, interviewing players, and watching them at pro days on college campuses. Every year during draft day, Division I football players, Championship Football Division players, and sometime even Division II and Division III players get drafted and invited to attend an NFL camp. Can you believe that a few players never even attended college, but they made an NFL team?

Eric Swann was a local boy born down the road from me in Pinehurst, North Carolina. Eric was 6 foot 5 inches and over 300 pounds. Swann was planning on playing college football at North Carolina State University, but he was ruled academically ineligible before his freshman year. Eric decided to play for a team in San Francisco that did not pay its players but instead helped them find paying jobs. Amazingly, he was selected by the Phoenix Cardinals in the first round (sixth overall) in the 1991 NFL draft, and he played in the NFL until the year 2000. He did not play a single game for a college before he got drafted!

I knew a fellow United States Merchant Marine Academy football player who got invited to a Carolina Panthers' training camp to try out for the team as a punter. If an NFL team can find a football player at USMMA, they can find you anywhere.

The name on the college jersey is irrelevant to the NFL team. They just want to know if you can play football. The name of the college where a person gets his or her undergraduate degree is also irrelevant for most business recruiters. The name of the college may get someone an interview, but it is always up the individual after that moment.

The *Wall Street Journal* recently ran an article called "The Top 25 Recruiter Picks" in which they surveyed the top business recruiters in the industry and had them rank whose graduates were the top-rated by recruiters. I recently asked my parents and my students to guess the names of colleges that were ranked on this list. I heard school names such as Duke, Harvard, Stanford, Columbia, and most of the Ivy League and other "prestigious" schools. In the article Jennifer Merritt even discusses how recruiters are moving away from elite private colleges. Below are the results from of the top 25 schools whose graduates were top-rated:

1. Pennsylvania State University
2. Texas A&M University
3. University of Illinois at Urbana-Champaign
4. Purdue University
5. Arizona State University
6. University of Michigan, Ann Arbor
7. Georgia Institute of Technology
8. University of Maryland, College Park
9. University of Florida
10. Carnegie Mellon University
11. Brigham Young University
12. Ohio State University
13. Virginia Polytechnic Institute and State University
14. Cornell University
15. University of California, Berkeley
16. University of Wisconsin, Madison
17. University of California, Los Angeles
18. Texas Tech
19. (tie)North Carolina State University, Raleigh
20. (tie) University of Virginia

21. Rutgers University, New Brunswick
22. University of Notre Dame
23. Massachusetts Institute of Technology
24. University of Southern California
25. (tie) Washington State University
26. (tie) University of North Carolina, Chapel Hill

A college degree means you are educated, but it does not mean you are smarter than someone who does not have a degree. We all know that Bill Gates did not graduate from Harvard! Getting a college degree signifies to an employer that you took the time to study for four or more years and that you were able to complete the task. Having a college degree might not be necessary to be successful in life, but it certainly gives you an advantage.

Remember that a college degree is like a bus ticket. This bus can be driven anywhere and can go wherever your heart desires. This bus signifies your future. However, to get on the bus, you need a ticket, and that ticket is your college diploma. Without the diploma, you can't get on the bus and you will have to wait in line until you get a ticket. It does not matter what it says on the ticket or where you got the ticket or even how much you paid for the ticket. The only thing that matters is if you have a ticket!

I am excited that you have read this far! I hope you are ready to get started because I have helped nearly a thousand families through the years. I think we should all leave a path or a trail behind for the common good of all. This is my trail that many have followed successfully for years. Follow my trail so we can make sure that college becomes an asset and not a liability. Follow the steps as I guide you through a simple step-by-step process so that you will not sacrifice your retirement monies and life savings on expensive retail college costs. This 800-pound "gorilla" of paying for college will be off your shoulders shortly!

CHAPTER 16

STEP 3: Find Your "WHY"

I believe that students should not begin their college search until they have sat down in a quiet room and thought about what they want their lives to look like in the future. I know that teenagers barely think ahead by the hour, much less a year; but I think it is important for them to start thinking this way.

One thing I have noticed throughout history is that all great people on this earth had a vision or a purpose. They lived their lives every day trying to achieve this purpose. They reflected on what they did and what they needed to do to achieve this vision. I like to call this purpose or vision a person's "WHY?"

If you don't know your "WHY," how is anyone going to help you get to where you want to go?

Sometimes I will ask students to think about what their Wikipedia page will say about them in the distant future. I ask them how Wikipedia will describe or answer these questions about them:

1. What was your life like?

2. What would you like or hope to be doing four years from now? Fifteen years from now? Forty years from now?

3. What specifically would you like to learn during your life—intellectually, financially, and spiritually?

4. How much money will you need to acquire to do these things? By when will you need this money?

5. What do you want your life to be like on a day-to-day basis after college? In 15 years?

These are just a few of the questions you might want to ask a child. Don't worry if the child is not able to answer all these questions. The exercise is to make sure he or she knows *WHY* he or she is going off to college.

By understanding and knowing their *intention*, students will then know **why** *they are going to college.* The answer to "why" is much more important than "where" or even "when" a child goes to college. The "WHY" gives a child the reason for going to college and staying in college to finish the job. Finding the "WHY" also helps a child to understand that the years people spend in college prepare them for the rest of their lives. College is not a destination but a tool to achieve one's life's purpose.

Children need to understand "WHY" they are going to college, because this is what they will need to keep them motivated when times get tough.

A mother told me a sad story about her oldest daughter who had quit college and was looking to transfer to another school. The daughter and her best friend from high school had decided to attend the same college. The best friend joined a sorority, and the two friends barely saw each other after the one joined her sorority. The woman's daughter stayed at the college for another year before deciding to transfer to a different school. This is a great example of a student who did not have her own answers to "WHY" she was going to college. Her "WHY" was that she wanted to go to the same college as her friend.

During the first two weeks in July at the United States Merchant Marine Academy in Kingspoint, NY, all freshmen go through indoctrination. The midshipman goes through a rigorous regime of physical, moral, and regiment training. The training is very demanding with little downtime for the new students. It requires mental, physical, and emotional steadfastness by the young men and women. This is the time when the upperclassmen and the drill sergeants try to weed out the students who really don't want to be at the academy. The upperclassmen never make any student quit. But they are like piranhas when they notice a mental weakness in a freshman. They will go after him or her "in waves" if there is any doubt that the freshman does not want to be at the academy or if he or she is at the academy for the wrong reason.

My first roommate at the academy left after the second day. He told me the first night we bunked together that the only reason he was at the academy was that his mother and father wanted him to be there. I found out later that his father was a United States congressman.

This young man went to the academy for the wrong reasons. When it got tough, he could not fall back on his "WHY" or the real reasons that he wanted to attend the academy.

Every student is going to be faced with some difficult times in college dealing with relationships, homesickness, friendships, academics, etc. Students will lean on their parents and on their "WHYs" to get them through the tough times.

The "WHYs" are the reasons a student decides to go to college. Until students find the reason why they want a college degree or why they would like to go to a certain college or why a college degree would help them achieve their goals and dreams, they will constantly look for an easier way. For example, we all know if we diet and exercise, we will eventually lose weight. But if we don't have a big enough answer to "WHY," we will not lose the excess weight and we will never achieve our goal because we will continue to look for an easier way. That is why diet pills and diet supplements are so popular. They promise you results without much work. The "WHYs" will give students the reasons to complete goals and go to college.

CHAPTER 17

STEP 4: Goal Planning to Pay for College

The number one goal for all college-bound families is for the student to graduate from college. This sounds like an easy goal, and I have never had parents come into my office and declare that their child was not going to graduate from college. Every parent assumes that his or her child will graduate from college. However, fewer than 60% of students graduate in six years.

Why is it so hard for a student to graduate from college? There are many factors: attending the wrong college, the cost of college, not knowing what to study, falling in love, etc. These are just a few of the reasons, and there are so many more.

When you visit a college, you will hear them tell you that college is the best investment that you will ever make for your child! While this is true, the colleges like to use the term "investment" because they want to make sure the parents understand that getting a degree is not guaranteed. In fact, it is just like purchasing any other investment: you pay up front and you could lose all your money.

Scott's father was the mayor of a local city. Scott was in the National Honors Society, was class president, and graduated first in his high school class. Scott was also all-conference linebacker for two years. While Scott was undersized and a little slow for his position, he gave it everything he could every time he went onto the field. Scott's dream was to play college football, and a few Division II schools had offered Scott an opportunity to play. Scott decided to attend a prestigious and expensive private college that gave him only a small amount of aid. During his first two years at college, Scott was doing great academically with a 3.4 GPA and was on pace to graduate in a little over a year. He loved playing football until one day he severely injured his knee. After surgery, the team doctor told Scott that it would take at least a year or longer for him to recover strength in his knee. He told Scott that his days of playing football might be over.

Out of the blue one night, Scott called his parents to inforr that he did not like the college anymore, that he could not play footbau anymore, that he could not stand being at the college, and that he wanted to quit and come home. His parents were obviously shocked, and they reminded Scott that he was doing great academically and that he was on pace to graduate in a little over a year and a half. Scott still insisted on quitting, but his parents told him that he was not going to quit college and that he was not coming home. He was going to gut the last year and a half out and graduate, end of discussion. After this telephone conversation with his parents, Scott was not motivated to go to class, and he was not motivated to study. Scott eventually came home.

I learned four important lessons from Scott and his family.

Lesson 1: Emotions Are Powerful. If the student does not want to do something or is not motivated, the parents have little control. As mentioned earlier, at this age most students base their decisions on emotions and not on rational thinking. Emotional thinking is 25 to 100 times more powerful than rational thinking.

Lesson 2: All Is Not Forgotten. When Scott came home from the college, his parents were extremely disappointed in him. They knew he had the ability to graduate from college, but Scott decided otherwise. Also, Scott was disappointed in his parents because they were not supporting his decision. To this day, the relationship between Scott and his parents is strained.

Lesson 3: Easy to Quit and Hard to Start. When Scott returned home, the first thing his parents asked was what his future plans were. Scott did not know, so his parents told him that he needed to get a job until he figured them out. Scott took a job selling cars at a local dealership. He started making some money, so he decided to move out of the house into a new apartment. Within six months, Scott purchased a new car, and within a year, he had a new girlfriend. The next year, I called Scott to see if he was ever going back to college. He told me that he was saving up his money so that when he returned to college, he would have some spending cash. It has been over five years! Scott has not been back to college and probably never will. Once you quit going to school and get out of the routine of studying and doing homework, it is very difficult to go back to school.

Lesson 4: College Can Be an Asset or a Liability. When I spoke with Scott's parents, they were heartbroken. They had $80,000 in Parent PLUS Loan debt that they would have to pay for the rest of their lives. The father told me, "It's like we paid for three years of summer camp costing $80,000. I have nothing to show for it, and neither does Scott. He can't even put it on his resume."

The mother then said, "The worst thing about this is that as I look at my bank statement every month and see the money being drafted out of our account to pay these college loans, it reminds me of Scott's failure to complete his college degree. It's like a dagger in the heart!"

I have to remind my parents, just like Scott, that if students are not motivated and they don't want to do something while they are in college, they will not do it. Parents are no longer around to make sure students are waking up in the morning to go to class. They are no longer around to limit their computer gaming time. They are no longer around to make sure they get off the phone so they can complete their homework. Screaming and threatening a student no longer works when a student is away from home (and probably did not work when they lived at home).

How do you make sure a student graduates from college? You have to give students some accountability through this process. You have to give them some responsibility and some "skin in the game."

The best way to do this is to get as much aid and free money as possible from the colleges to reduce the cost of college. If there is any "gap" or money that we still need to come up with to pay for college, I suggest my parents take out loans in the child's name to cover this cost. The parents can then save money while the student is in college so that they can pay off as much of these loans as possible after the student graduates from college.

Goal #1: The Carrot and the Stick

I call this next step the "carrot and the stick." The carrot is the money that you will save to help the student pay off his or her college loan. The stick is the loan in the child's name (cosigned by the parents). If the child decides he or she wants to quit college, then the child is responsible for paying the loan. If the child graduates, the parents help him or her pay off these loans.

Just like most parents would not pay a child before he or she completes a chore, I suggest parents do not pay the student before his or her college is complete. Parents need to make getting a college degree like completing a job. "Pay in" is not rendered until the job is done.

Some parents are concerned about the interest accumulating on the student loans, and they should be concerned. To help reduce these concerns, I suggest to my parents that they implement two strategies to help mitigate the accumulating interest.

1. Strategy 1: Pay just the interest on the loan while the student is in college. Do not pay off the entire loan, or there is no skin in the game.

2. Strategy 2: Save money in an account specifically set up to help pay off student loans after graduation. The interest in the account should be the same or close to the interest that the student loan is charging.

Goal #2: HEART and CALCULATOR

Sometimes I like to call this "fit and affordable," but I think "heart and calculator" has a better ring. The college selection must fit the student's and the parents' criteria. It must be a good fit socially and academically. If not, more than likely the student will not enjoy his or her time at the college and will return home.

Just as important as the fit, the college has to be affordable for the family. Parents should expect their child to get a great college education without going broke! It is very easy for parents to use all their life's savings to pay for their children's education if they decide on a college that is too expensive. If the college is not affordable, the parents should disregard this option and look at other, more affordable alternatives that the student found to be a good fit.

The first step in the college selection process is for students to identify their career goals! Over 60% of all college freshmen have no career planning or career goals. More importantly, research by the U.S. Department of Education concluded that the risk of students switching majors, taking extra years to graduate, transferring to another college, or even dropping out of college surges significantly if the student does not complete any career goal training prior to selecting a college. In fact, *the Department of Education research shows that 51% of students leave the college in which they originally enrolled.* If parents want to reduce the cost of college and have huge tuition savings, they must start by having their children complete a career assessment study.

When I started at the United States Merchant Marine Academy, I had no idea what major I wanted to study. Like most young men and women, I knew what things I liked to do and what subjects in school I did not like. At the time I was in school, there were only two majors open to me: engineer and "deckie," or ship management. I picked engineer because I was good at math and because my brother was studying to be an engineer as well, but I didn't put much effort into figuring out what I really wanted to study before entering the academy.

Fortunately, I had the opportunity to experience what a career in the Navy would be like while I was still in school by sailing on a Naval Destroyer. In addition, I spent many months sailing on a merchant ship while in college, giving me a brief view of what a career as a merchant sailor would be like. I also was afforded the unique opportunity to intern at a small ship-building company in Louisiana right before my senior year in college performing duties of a marine engineer. While I enjoyed these experiences and certainly each of these remarkable experiences helped me to grow in many ways, more than anything I learned that a career in the Navy, as a merchant sailor, and as a marine engineer was not the career path for me.

I did graduate with a marine systems engineering degree from the academy, but I was lucky to be able to have actual hands-on experience with a variety of potential careers before I graduated. Not many students are able to do this, and it really helped me know the direction I wanted to take after graduation. I ended up working for one of the largest international shipping companies called Sea-Land Inc.

It took me many more years of soul-searching to find my passion to help families with college. However, I wish I could have known before I went off to college what careers or majors would have been a good fit for me based upon my personality and my skillset.

Josh was a mountain of a boy. He stood 6 foot 5 inches tall and weighed close to 280 pounds. One day I asked him why he wanted to study business management in college, and he told me he wanted to run a restaurant when he graduated from college. After further questioning, I found out that the only reason he wanted to own a restaurant was because he loved to eat! Josh was very intelligent, and based upon the career and aptitude testing we perform at Clark College Funding, Inc., I knew he was a very outgoing person. But after speaking with him, I found out what was really important to him.

He told me that his goal in life was to have a family and to work in a small town. He really didn't care if he owned a restaurant or worked in the local bank as long as he could live where he desired and have the family life he wanted. Initially, I was under the impression that he wanted to own a restaurant because he liked that line of business, but I now knew that he believed that owning and running a restaurant was the best way for him to achieve his goals of having a family and living in a small town.

Josh's "WHY" to go to college was so he could have the lifestyle of owning his own business in a small town and raising a family. Next, we gave Josh a career aptitude test that helped him narrow down his college major. Josh went on to graduate in four years from a local college with honors. Knowing "WHY" Josh wanted to go to college gave him the reason for attending college and knowing what he should study before entering college gave him the focus to graduate in only four years. To find out more about great career aptitude tests, please visit my Web site at **www.collegeaidformiddleclass.com**.

If your child is in high school, he or she should perform some type of aptitude test or career search. Students need to know what careers are available to them, and they need to know all the careers that fit their skills and personality. They need to identify occupations matching their personal attributes. The students also need to know that there are a large number of careers that they will like, enjoy, and excel in doing. Students find it exciting to know that they have so many possibilities. I don't think you will find "the one career" that the student will want to do for the rest of his or her life, but I do think you can see trends in the result. These trends will help you narrow down the student's college choices to ones that have the careers or majors in which the student is interested.

This is also a good time to have your child think about what he or she wants his or her life to look like in 10, 20, or even 30 years. Have him or her think of the type of lifestyle he or she would like to have.

A New Age

Old Rule: Pick a major that is suitable to a lifetime career in one field or position (e.g., nurse, accountant, teacher, etc.).

New Rule: One is almost expected to change jobs frequently in the marketplace, and it is perfectly acceptable to pursue a completely new career.

In the late 1990s, AOL was at the leading edge to the Internet, and many people wanted to work for AOL. Today Google and Apple Inc. are the fashionable technology companies to work for. Who knows what startup companies will be changing the world 10 years from today? In this dynamic world of changing careers and changing technology, it is essential to get a good all-around education that will prepare a student for the changes in the future.

With the old rule of picking a major that was relevant 30 years ago, if you graduated with a general business degree, you hoped for a long career with one company like IBM, GE, or Xerox. However, today with many people and CEOs working until they are 80 years old, you can easily change careers and be successful.

The thought of having to pick a major intimidates some students because they think they will be stuck in the major or waste valuable time in a major they might not want to pursue. Even if students get a degree in a field they do not necessarily want to work in for the rest of their lives, they have the opportunity to reinvent themselves by starting new careers throughout their lifetimes. The old rule of finding a job with one company and working at that same company until you retire no longer applies. It is never too late to change your mind or start over.

However, students should still try to reduce the chance of changing majors as much as possible. By constantly changing majors, students drastically increase their amount of time in college. Completing a good career and aptitude test will help a student narrow down the majors that will be a good fit for his or her particular skillset and personality. Research from America's Career Research Network Association and the U.S. Department of Education found that students who complete career planning before college:

1. Graduate on time
2. Have fewer transfers and major changes
3. Are more goal-focused and motivated
4. Have higher academic achievement

Also, students should make certain to think seriously about what they want their lives to look like and the lifestyle they would like to have 10, 20, or even 30 years from today. For example, if a student plans on being a social worker after college, he or she might also want to think about the lifestyle that goes along with being a social worker. Most social workers work long hours and become emotionally invested in their work. Social work can be very rewarding, but the pay is not always great. The student would need to make sure he or she is comfortable with that lifestyle before deciding to pursue social work.

If a student is undecided about his or her career goals or major, the family may want to look for colleges and universities that have a "first year college (FYC)" program. For example, at NC State University, the school advises students through their first year at the university with career advising and one-on-one academic counseling. All students in FYC are required to take "Introduction to University Education" for two semesters. During the classes, the students discuss their personal goals and values and then use this information to make sensible, knowledgeable conclusions about their undergraduate majors and the exploration of careers at NC State. At the end of their first year, students should have enough information about themselves and the university to make informed decisions about the right major.

Albert Einstein said, "A person does not need to go to college to learn facts. He can learn them from books. The value of a liberal arts college education is that it trains the mind to think." If a student is still unsure of what he or she wants to do or study, he or she may consider attending a liberal arts college. "Liberal arts" does not mean a student has to be liberal or be interested in the arts. Students can study math, engineering, and physics at a liberal arts college. Attending a liberal arts college, however, can teach students how to think. A good Web site to visit is www.collegenews.org/theannapolisgroup.xml. The Annapolis Group is an organization of liberal arts colleges.

In most cases, a career unfolds as one's life progresses. Very few people actually plan a career. When I spent my year on various sailing vessels, I learned some important lessons in life. One of the first things I learned is that sailors have a different perspective on life than non-sailors. When you sail a ship on the ocean, it is almost impossible to follow a straight line to get to your next destination due to the constant changing of the elements. One's career is very much like sailing on a ship, because you will be forced to make adjustments to your plan. Sometimes the wind will be at your stern and push you towards your goals, but sometimes you will be faced with challenges that might push you off your route. As long as you know where you are going and you have the will and the fortitude, you will eventually get to your destination!

Very few people actually plan a career. However, by exploring and examining one's skills, interests, and personality today, it can give one a "leg up" on the future. Also, the students should try to distinguish between what they are good at doing and what they enjoy doing. I tell students always to focus on what they enjoy doing, because they have the rest of their lives to work. Very few people in the world actually enjoy going to work every day. Life is too short not to enjoy your work.

Below are a few ideas to help find your career goals:

1. If you have a career in mind, read as much as possible about the career. If you think you want to be an air traffic controller, go online and search "air traffic controller." Go to www.wikipedia.com, where you can see most any career described and profiled. You

might also look online or in the library to see if there are any trade magazines about your career.

2. Shadowing a professional or even talking to someone in the field will give you a better understanding of the job. For example, try to speak with an actual air traffic controller or try to arrange a time to take a tour of the air traffic control tower. You might want to ask about the best colleges to study to become an air traffic controller or where most of the people you shadowed attended. You might discover colleges that specialize in this industry that you did not even know existed. Try to find out what they like about their job and what they don't like about the job.

3. Go to a library or your guidance department and obtain the U.S. Department of *Labor's Dictionary of Occupational Titles (DOT)*. Research the various occupations under each (three letter) listing using the **DOT Number** as a reference. This will provide you with a basic idea of the job specifications.

4. You might want to take the Campbell Interest and Skill Survey. It costs about $20 and can be taken online at www.profiler.com.

5. A good site to consider is www.mycoolcarreer.com. It has self-assessment tools and videos of careers.

6. Another good source is the Holland and Self-directed Career Search at www.selfdirectsearch.com for $4.95, or you can get a paper copy by calling 800-331-8378. (When you call, ask for SDS Form R Professional Report Service Sample Kit. The cost is $15.)

Other books to consider for further research:

1. *College to Career*, J. S. Mitchell: The College Board
2. *100 Best Careers For The 21st Century*, S. Field: Prentice Hall
3. *The Encyclopedia of Career and Vocational Guidance*, W. E. Hopke: Ferguson Publishing
4. *Professional Careers Sourcebook*, K. M. Savage: Gale Research

5. *What Color is Your Parachute?*, R. N. Bolles: Ten Speed Press
6. *Occupational Outlook Handbook*, U.S. Department of Labor: U.S. Govt. Printing Office

Web sites to consider for further research:

1. VARK
   www.vark-learn.com

2. Career Interests Game www.career.missouri.edu

3. U.S. News and World Report: College Personality Quiz
   http://colleges.usnews.rankingsandreviews.com/best-colleges

4. Career Services Center, University of Waterloo
   www.cdm.uwaterloo.ca

5. Keirsey Temperament Scale
   www.keirsey.com

6. Occupational Outlook Handbook
   www.bls.gov/oco

7. Major Resource Kits www.udel.edu/CSC/mrk.html

CHAPTER 18

STEP 5: Clarify What You Want: Family College Standards

Once you have a better idea of what your child would like to study in college, it is time to start using the channel approach to narrow down the college choices. To do this, you must know which colleges to eliminate and which colleges to keep! It is time to clarify what you want in a college experience and to identify what is not important in a college. In other words, you need to identify your college standards and criteria. A family's college standard is a very clear statement on the criteria a college must have in order to achieve the student's career goals and to help him or her to achieve his or her purpose.

After working with hundreds of families, I have found that the criteria parents are looking for in a college and the criteria students are looking for in a college are sometimes completely different. Parents need to realize that what they like in a college is not necessarily what their children might be looking for. To eliminate any confusion and to bring my students' and parents' standards together, I find it helpful to distinguish the similarities and the differences. Once we know the similarities and the differences in the parents' and students' standards, we can begin discussing those factors that are most important to both the parents and the children.

Below is a list of 29 criteria that you can use to help distinguish the most important benchmarks. This is certainly not a complete list of standards, but it will give you an idea of what you should be considering.

1. **Academic programs:** Will the course of study provide the required academic experience?
   - Consider the availability of capstone, learning communities, study abroad, service learning, research/creative projects, and internships.

2. **Major:** Does the school have the student's major?

3. **Location:** Is the location of this college satisfactory to your student's needs?

4. **Size:** Is the size of this college satisfactory?
   - *Small:* less than 3,000 students
   - *Medium:* between 3,000 and 10,000 students
   - *Medium Large:* between 10,000 and 20,000 students
   - *Large:* greater than 20,000 students

5. **Athletic program:** Does this college have a sports program that meets the student's needs (as an athlete or a spectator)?

6. **Talent program:** Does this college have a talent program that meets the student's needs (theater, newspaper, debate team)?

7. **Special programs:** Does this college have special programs or facilities that the student needs or must have (learning disabilities, special medical facilities, etc.)?

8. **Co-op programs:** Does this college have an academic co-op (study/work) program *in the student's major* that can reduce your college costs and help the student achieve employment after graduation?

9. **Job placement:** Does this college have a placement office that places a high number of students in jobs *prior* to graduation?

10. **Religion:** Does this college have a religious program that fits the child's needs?

11. **Attrition:** Does this college have a high number of freshmen that graduate within five years?

12. **Student/faculty ratio:** Does this college have a low student-to-faculty ratio to guarantee more interactive classroom participation and personal faculty attention for the student?

13. **Faculty with PhDs:** Does this college have a high number of faculty with PhDs?

14. **Tutoring:** Does the college have a system to help struggling students?

15. **Campus setting:** Is this college located in a desirable area or neighborhood? Does it have the right "feel"?

16. **Safety:** Does this college's campus have adequate security and a good safety reputation?

17. **Alcohol/drug policy:** Self-explanatory.

18. **Student body reputation:** Does this college's student body reputation fit the student's personality?

19. **Diversity:** Does the student mix at this college fit the student's personality or desire for cultural growth?

20. **Greek system**: Does the role that fraternities and sororities play at this college fit the student's needs?

21. **Housing:** Is this college's housing (and housing policy) satisfactory? Are the Internet and other connectivity readily available?

22. **Food:** Is the on-campus food at this college satisfactory to your student's needs?

23. **Weather:** Is this college located in a climate that is satisfactory to your student's needs?

24. **Cost:** What is the cost of attendance?

25. **Financial aid:** What are the available awards, need and merit money, etc.?

26. **Prestige:** Will the university fit the student's or parents' expectations? Will it help in the job search?

27. **Accreditation:** Does the university or college have the proper certification? Can the student transfer community college credits to this university if needed?

28. **Retention and persistence**: Do students "vote with their feet" after the freshman year? How quickly do students finish their education?

29. **Prerequisites for freshman enrollment:** Will your student need to have additional academic preparation prior to enrollment?

I suggest that you take the list above and make a grid *or go to my Web site at www.collegeaidformiddleclass.com* to download an Excel spreadsheet with the above information already on it to save you time.

You and your child should go into separate rooms and place numbers beside each benchmark that you feel strongly about. You probably only need to mark your top five criteria in order of importance with "1" being your most important factor and "5" being your least important factor. You will probably find that the results between the student and the parent are different. That is okay, because you will use this list to discuss the differences and find the common ground.

After you have discussed the differences and the similarities, you need to merge the two lists into one final list. This is **your family's college standards!** It will guide you and help clarify what your family has determined to be the most important factors in a college. Once you know your college standards, the channeling process is easy!

CHAPTER 19

STEP 6: Channeling: Top-down Approach

When I meet with my students and parents for the first time, I ask them what colleges they are interested in and why they picked these schools. Below is my students' list of why they often pick a particular college:

1. My girlfriend is going to apply to the school.
2. My boyfriend is going to apply.
3. All of my friends are going to apply to the college.
4. Good sports teams
5. Good location (e.g., close to the beach)

Parents, I am not going to let you off the hook either. I ask my parents why they want their child to attend a certain college, and below are the typical answers I usually receive from the parents:

1. Money (usually top priority)
2. Money (second in priority)
3. Money (Cost of college is a major concern.)
4. The parent went to that college, so they believe it will be a perfect fit for their child.
5. It is within two hours' driving distance from home. (A lot of mothers have this concern.)
6. Window sticker: They believe this is a great college based upon what they hear from other parents, and they believe if the child graduates from the college, it will impress others.

College is an expensive investment for families. In most cases, it is the second largest investment a family will make other than purchasing a home. Think of college like buying a new car every year. A family will probably spend anywhere from $15,000 to $60,000 a year! I think you will agree that if you are spending this much money on a college investment, the above list is the wrong way to pick a school.

I would love for my students to say the following when I ask them why they wanted to attend a particular college.

> "I'd love to attend ___ University. It's a great opportunity for me to study ___. In fact, this university is well-known for its outstanding faculty and is credited for being one of the best universities at which to study ___. And, by the way, they offer the best financial aid package in comparison to their short list of competitors."

The first sentence, "I'd love to attend XXX University" implies that the students have done some homework into the school. If they enjoy the experience, they'll have a better chance of graduating.

The second sentence, "It's a great opportunity to study XXX" implies that students understand what they want to do once they have graduated and that they have completed a career assessment to guide them.

"In fact, this university is well-known for its outstanding faculty and it is credited for being one of the best universities at which to study XXX" lets me know that the students have researched the school and found that the institution pours a lot of resources into their major. Most students and parents make the mistake of thinking that because a particular university has a good overall reputation, every major inside of that university or college gets equal billing when it comes to resources. That is usually not the case, so when you go on your college visits, make sure you speak with someone in the department at which your student will be studying. Let me put this another way: Some colleges have big buildings for business majors and little buildings for accounting majors. Other colleges have big buildings for accounting majors and little buildings for business majors. If you are a business major, you will want to go to the college with the big business building.

"Best financial aid in comparison…" Did you know that some colleges will compete for students? We'll see an example of this later on.

Another mistake most students and parents make during the college selection process is that they pick one or two schools that they think they like and try to add a few more colleges to the list that they think they might want to attend.

We see students start with a list of two or three colleges and try to build their list out from there. The "filler colleges" are probably schools that the student is not really interested in attending. Most of the time with the "filler colleges," the students will not finish the applications because of lack of interest. If the student does complete the application, it is usually rushed and any essays are not very well-written. What happens? The student is then left with a list of three to four colleges to select from instead of the 6 to 10 that I recommend because the "filler" colleges can see by the application that the student is not really interested. The student now has fewer choices and ultimately less leverage with each college.

By starting with two or three schools and adding filler colleges, the students are making a huge mistake! We are blessed in the United States to have such a variety and abundance of colleges and universities. Most students and parents are familiar with only a very small portion of these schools. Many students and parents don't know about all the great colleges and universities that would be a perfect fit, and they do not even know that these colleges exist.

The better approach to selecting a college is called the "top-down approach." You need to use the top-down approach to narrow down your schools because you will identify all the schools that would be a good fit for a student, even the schools that you did not know before starting the college search.

There are over 6,500 colleges, universities, technical institutes, and vocational training institutes in the United States and many more if you include Canada. To put this in perspective, there are 110 colleges and universities just in the state of North Carolina, and I know my parents who live in North Carolina are not familiar with all the colleges that are in this state.

Once you have narrowed down the major the student wants to study and you have merged the parents' and student's most important criteria for selecting a college, you can begin the top-down approach to narrow your college selection from 6,500 plus institutions down to initially 25 to 40 colleges. Don't be alarmed if you do not recognize all the names of the colleges and universities from your initial list.

Think of this initial funneling down like parents taking a daughter shopping to purchase a new prom dress. When the family enters the store, they notice that the clothing shop has over 6,000 dresses that would fit their daughter and it seems overwhelming. They will need to find a dress that she will love and a dress that is affordable for the parents.

So the parents tell their daughter to find out the most important criteria or what she would like to see in the dress (length, color, style, etc.). Once they know the criteria on the type of dress they are looking for, the daughter and the parents are now able to eliminate 99% of the dresses by the length, color, and style fairly quickly. The family will end up with approximately 25 to 40 dresses that make the initial cut. Now the dress selection is not overwhelming to the parents or their daughter because they can really take their time to look at the remaining dresses. But if they did not take the time before they started shopping to determine the criteria or to know what they are looking for in a dress, then the family would waste a lot of time and probably a lot of money on a dress that the daughter might not really like.

Much like the college selection process, parents and students need to start with a career/aptitude test and then combine their most important criteria before they begin narrowing down the colleges so the family can easily reduce the colleges down to a reasonable number to look at in detail.

Out of the 25 to 40 dresses, there are some "name brand" labels on the dresses that the family will automatically recognize, and there are some dress labels that the daughter likes just as much but is not familiar with. If the daughter likes the color, the size, the length, and the look of the dress, she should still keep it under consideration even though she is not familiar with the dress label.

If the daughter told the sales clerk when entering the store that she only wanted dresses from specific dress designers, her dress selection would have been very limited and she might have missed out on the perfect dress.

If families can determine what they are looking for in a college, they need to write it down so that all family members know what is most important. Next, use this information to narrow down college choices using all 6,500 plus colleges and universities. The results will probably leave you with anywhere from 20 to 100 colleges. If your college list has less than 20, you need to remove at least one criterion so that more colleges are on your initial list. For example, a family might be looking for a small, private college with less than 8,000 students, located in the southeast, and situated in a small town that has a major in engineering. This result might only find you five colleges. That is not enough, so the family might need to look at colleges not only in the southeast, but also in the south and the north to get the desired number of colleges. Having at least 20 colleges initially is very beneficial, because the next step will greatly reduce your college selections.

On the other hand, if your result has more than 100 colleges, you might want to be a little more specific or add more criteria to reduce the number of college choices to 100 or less.

CHAPTER 15

STEP 7: Collect the College Numbers and Compare to College Selection

"Not everything that counts can be counted,
and not everything that can be counted counts."
– sign hanging in Einstein's office at Princeton

Colleges and universities use the student's GPA, SAT/ACT score, and community service hours to tell a story about the student. Much like words, numbers can also tell a story. It helps a college find out where a student has been, where they are right now, and where they want to go.

To play this college planning game right, the first thing a student and family must do is figure out where they are today and compare this to the averages from your college selection. This means taking an honest look at your GPA, SAT/ACT score, and community service hours. It may sound difficult and even scary, but it is a simple process that must be completed.

If you are like me, there have been times in my life when I did not want to go on the scale to see my weight. I wrongly told myself not to go on the scale so that I would not have to look at how much weight I have gained. I eventually came to my senses and decided that if I did not go on the scale, I could not get an accurate measurement of my weight in order to set a course to reduce my weight.

Many students do not want to collect their college numbers because, like me, they don't want to step on the scale to face reality. The intention of this step is not to make students feel guilty for having a less-than-stellar GPA or not performing well on their standardized test. Don't fret over things you can't change now, but work towards charting a course for the future!

When a college admissions committee assembles to review piles of student transcripts, they will spend no more than 15 minutes on every application. They will first eliminate those students who do not have the minimum college numbers. For example, a college could have the following as their minimum:

GPA	SAT I	ACT	Community Service Hours
3.0	1650 (1150 w/o writing)	24	100

We will begin to compare the student's college numbers to the results of your college selection in **step 10**. This will give the family a clearer idea of exactly where a student stands when a college or university reviews your application and will give you a starting point for narrowing down colleges for which your child would be a good fit academically. For now, just collect the student's college numbers and write them down. As the student takes the SAT and ACT, make sure you update the college numbers.

CHAPTER 21

STEP 8: Purge Your List Using Emotional Intelligence and F.E.A.R.

"Another form of insanity is the use of opinions instead of facts."
– Robert Kiyosaki

The reason that families I work with get great financial aid award letters and attend great colleges is not because their students are academically smarter or did better on the SAT. One of the main reasons they get great results is because of emotional intelligence! I have been told that your emotions are 25 times more powerful than rational decision making. I think this number is low. When someone gets mad and loses his or her temper, his or her emotions are probably a million times stronger than rational decision making. Haven't we all regretted saying something in an argument after we said it or hastily replied to an e-mail out of emotion?

Many families fail in this college planning process because they have no control over their emotions. Believe me, picking a college is a very, very emotional time for the parents and the students because money is involved. Money, as we all know, is a very emotional subject. FEAR is the leading factor that causes us to lose emotional intelligence, especially when choosing a college.

FEAR:
> F – False
> E – Evidence
> A – Appearing
> R – Real

The relationship between FEAR and fact-finding is a delicate balance for most individuals. The more facts, numbers, and ratios that you can uncover, the less you will fear. With less FEAR and more facts, you will be able to make an informed opinion. Forming your own opinions on a college will eventually eliminate most FEAR. *However, when families do not do their own fact-finding,* **FEAR** *is more prevalent and these families rely on the opinions of others.* They gather their information from what other parents say, from what other students tell them, and from the various college publications and Web sites that are heavily weighted on opinions of others.

Can a family conquer these FEARs to become emotionally intelligent? Are you strong enough to take a look at yourself in the mirror to make sure you are not one of the many that are using false evidence appearing real?

1. **FEAR of choice:** Many students make the mistake of getting their heart set on one college. They believe that there is only one college or university that is perfect for them. In reality, there are dozens, if not hundreds, of colleges where students will thrive if they search hard enough. You will find that there is not much difference between many of the schools selected, and you can always find more if you open your mind to the possibilities.

2. **FEAR of prestige:** Many families believe that getting into a "big name school" with the proper rankings from *U.S. News & World Report* is important. While rankings might help you see the few unique differences among the schools, these rankings constantly change, and more importantly they do not indicate where an individual student might feel comfortable. Opinions from so-called experts greatly influence the results of the rankings. Use this information as a resource, but use your own opinions to rank the colleges.

3. **FEAR of social acceptance:** Many parents and students speak among themselves about colleges and their impressions of the various schools. That in itself is not bad, but basing your entire belief about a college on what friends think or the impressions of

others is a road to failure. If you base your entire college selection on what other people tell you, you will make a tragic mistake because your judgment about a college will already be tainted. A great example of this is if your family and another family go to the same restaurant, at the same time, on the same day, and order the exact same meal. The other family comes away with a bad impression of the restaurant even though the food was excellent because their waiter was rude. On the other hand, your impression of the restaurant was very good because your waitress was wonderful and the food was good. If a mutual friend asks both families about their opinions of the restaurant, they will receive two different opinions. Listen to what others say, but form your own opinions by allowing each college to start with a clean slate before forming your own opinions.

4. **FEAR of new friendships:** Many students pick colleges based on where their friends (including boyfriends and girlfriends) are applying because they fear going to a new school and trying to find new friends. This is not usually an issue for families that move often, because the child has adapted to new schools and new friends in the past. But for a child that has had the same group of friends since he or she was in kindergarten, this is a big obstacle. If a student has great friends in high school, no matter where each friend attends college or moves, they will always be friends. If the family performs an intelligent college search with many good options, the student will meet friends almost immediately because many of the students will have the same interest. The student will be able to keep up with high school friends with the different forms of social media and texting. It is also fun to visit high school friends at other colleges.

5. **FEAR of letting go:** Many parents will tell me that they do not want their child more than two hours' driving distance away from home. In some cases, this is necessary because the child might not be emotionally ready or may have special needs, so it is important that he or she stay closer to home. However, many

parents conjure up this fear because they are afraid of letting go (especially if it's the first child). Children leaving home and going off to college is a big step for all families, and separation anxiety is difficult for everyone involved. Nevertheless, this is part of the process of letting your children become young adults and allowing them to mature. This is their time to make friends on their own, pay their own bills, do their laundry, wake up in the morning to go to class, etc. In some cases, parents inadvertently slow the child's maturation progression by being so close to their child's college. Parents, if the student wants to stay close to home, by all means please encourage him or her to do so. But please don't limit the child's college selection if he or she is okay with being farther away from home. Your child will always love you, and most of the time he or she will be a little homesick when he or she first leaves. Let the students spread their wings, and you will enjoy watching them blossom into mature young adults over the next few years.

6. **FEAR of failure:** We have been taught since childhood that failing at something is wrong and that we should avoid making mistakes at all cost. Robert Kiyosaki once said, "People that are afraid of losing, they wind up losing. Losing is the part of the process of winning." Sometimes parents try to keep students close to home to try to protect them from making mistakes. This is the job of a parent, and you will continue to have this job for the rest of your life. As parents, we have all taught our children the difference between right and wrong, and we have all passed on our morals to our children. During college, it is up to the child to follow the moral guidelines that you have taught them. In some cases, the students will make judgment mistakes during college. Allow them to make these mistakes, because finding out what they did wrong and avoiding this behavior in the future is sometimes the best way to learn. Recently, a mother told me that she would not even visit a college with her daughter because another parent told her that this college was a party school. I had to inform this parent

that all colleges can be party schools if the student looks hard enough for one. It is up the student to make these decisions when he or she is at college, and you have to trust your student to make the right choices or learn from his or her mistakes.

Just think about a professional baseball player in the MLB. They became professional players by practicing a lot. Most have been practicing hitting a baseball since they were children, but the majority of these MLB players cannot hit the ball 3 out of 10 times when they play the game. If a baseball player had a batting average of .300 consistently, he would be in the MLB hall of fame. That is only succeeding 3 out of 10 times and failing 7 out of 10 times! Failure is normal and necessary for learning. The key to learning in life is learning from your failure and not repeating your mistakes.

7. **FEAR of lack of name recognition:** I try to convince my families that the most famous colleges and universities are not necessarily the best for their child. Sometimes trying to convince students and parents of this is almost impossible. Just because a college or university is well-known due to its collegiate athletic programs or because it is an Ivy League school does not mean the school has a better academic reputation among business recruiters and graduate school admissions staff. In the long run, where you attended college is not as important as what you learned while you were in college.

8. **FEAR of "the final decision":** While picking a college can have significant impact on a student's future, it probably will not be the most important decision a student will ever make. What is inside each individual, and not where he or she attended college, is most important.

9. **FEAR that a child will not be pushed academically:** Some families believe that if their student is in the top 25% of the incoming freshman class, the student will not be challenged academically because he or she is already more advanced than his or her peers. However, the student will find that he or she is surrounded by like-

minded students that are very bright, intelligent, and competitive. Conversely, by picking only colleges in which a student is in the top 25%, you are ensuring that the academic work will not be too difficult for the student. I have had students attend colleges in which they were in the bottom 25% academically, and most struggled or were burnt out after their sophomore year because they spent all their downtime in the library or studying late into the evenings just to maintain a passable GPA. Most of these students end up transferring after a few years because they did not enjoy themselves while they were in college. Also, students who are doing well academically in college are usually the ones who are offered the best co-ops and internships. As you know, businesses like students who build up their resume while in college. In addition, many colleges now have honors programs. These honors programs are designed for students with superior academic records. The honors programs offer opportunities for individualized study, special classes, and other unique intellectual and social activities. This is a wonderful opportunity for the student to be treated like an MVP by the college and be pushed academically as well. Why not take advantage of this special offer?

Does it really matter how many books are in the library or how many faculty members have PhDs? This tells you nothing about their teaching ability! Researchers have shown that the more engaging a college, the more students learn. In other words, the quality of an undergraduate education is determined by the variety of educationally sounds activities inside and outside the classroom. The more feedback the students receive in problem solving and writing, the more proficient they become.

If you choose to believe that the name of a college or the lack of name recognition of a college will dictate the quality of education, then this will become your reality. However, if you believe that it is most important to find a college based upon meeting the student's college standards, this will become your reality. Choose your ideas very carefully, because your ideas become your reality!

How do you conquer these fears and become emotionally intelligent? I cannot tell you that, but I would suggest starting *by looking only at* *facts, gathering and compiling research about a particular school, and using your own personal judgments to formulate the list of schools to which you will apply.*

Don't consider others' opinions about a college until you have had a chance to evaluate the college yourself with facts about the school, to see how it meets the criteria you set for yourself, and to visit the college to make sure it meets these benchmarks. Each institute you are evaluating should start with a clean slate without the influence of marketing material and peer opinion or gossip. Use an analytical approach to help you narrow down your schools.

CHAPTER 21

STEP 9: Know the Facts and Gather Information

"Your fears have no basis in fact."
– Unknown

A fact is a truth learned through actual experience or observation of something known to be true. Knowing the facts about the college will help you become emotionally intelligent and overcome most fears about a college. Gathering facts about a college does not mean looking at college rankings because these rankings are flawed and based upon perception. For example, the magazine *U.S. News & World Report: America's Best Colleges* is a wonderful reference. Many students and parents hold the rankings in this magazine in high regard. However, an astonishing 25% of the schools' rankings are based on the *reputation of the schools.* Each year, the magazine surveys college administrators and asks them to rank schools based upon their *opinions.* How much do you think a school administrator in a college in West Virginia knows about a school in North Dakota? I would bet not much.

Many of my students and parents use Fiske Guide to Colleges as a reference. I suggest my parents read it as a reference only because the authors of the book collect information about the various schools through questionnaires that are completed by the school administrators and a cross section of students. Can you see a flaw in this system? These are not facts but opinions from the school's own administration and students. How critical do you think they will be?

Fiske Guide to Colleges, U.S. News & World Report, Princeton Review's The Best 366 Colleges, and other publications like them are all good references. But the only facts you can find in these books are grade point averages and SAT or ACT scores.

You need to begin by collecting the facts about the college. The process of fact-finding will help you make up your own opinion about a college. You can begin by looking at the school's Common Data Set. The Common Data Set (CDS) is data that colleges collect each year about graduation rate, freshman class profile, student retention, and important financial aid statistics, among other things. The CDS was an effort between the colleges and the College Board, *U.S. News & World Report*, and Peterson's to standardize the data for these publications so that they could report the figures in their publications. The CDS is standardized among all schools, so you should see the same format at all the schools. You can easily find the CDS if you search for it on the college's Web site or type it in any search engine. You might even want to print the CDS to review.

To help with your college selection, I suggest you start by gathering the facts and information below:

1. Understand the Mission Statement

By reading each college's mission statement and strategic plan, you will gain insight about the goals of the school, its purpose, and the type of student the school wants to recruit. You will be able to read about the values of the school and how the college might challenge the student. You might find the qualifications and background information of the faculty that the college tries to recruit and certain studies or disciplines that the school emphasizes. A student should make sure his or her individual goals and values are in alignment with the college's. For example, a family that is looking for a college with strong Christian beliefs should read the college's mission statement to see if the college holds to those values. In addition, if the college states that it is focusing on creating a more diverse campus or would like to attract more out-of-state students, then this gives you insight into its future goals and where a student might fit with these goals. You should be able to find both the mission statement and/or the strategic plan on the college's Web site.

2. Find 25th, Median, and 75th Percentile Score for SAT or ACT

Knowing these numbers is invaluable, because a family will need to be able to compare the student's "college numbers" that you collected in step 7. Below is information taken directly from Wake Forest University's common data set. Wake Forest is one of the few colleges that does not require a student to submit an SAT or ACT score with his or her application. While these tests are optional on the application, of the students who submitted test scores in 2009, 68% of the freshman submitted SAT scores and 39% submitted ACT scores.

Percent submitting SAT scores: 68%
Percent submitting ACT scores: 39%

	25 Percentile	75 Percentile
SAT Critical Reading	580	690
SAT Math	600	700
Total SAT	1180	1390
ACT Composite	27	31

Of the students who submitted the scores, an SAT score of 1180 (math plus reading) was the 25th percentile. This means that 25% of the students who applied to Wake and submitted an SAT score had a score of 1180 or below. The 75th percentile means that 75% of Wake applicants submitting SAT scores had a score of 1390 or below. The median SAT and ACT scores are often on the CDS as well, but it was not indicated on Wake Forest's applications. However, this number can be found at www.CollegeResults.org. For Wake Forest, the median SAT verbal is 655 and median SAT math is 670 for a total median score of 1325.

25th Percentile	Median	75th Percentile
1180	1325	1390

A variation of +/- 100 points of the median is a good indication of a typical student. These are very important numbers and crucial to your success in narrowing down colleges. We will use this number in our next step to narrow down the colleges even further.

3. Graduation Rate in Four, Five, and Six Years

When a family is spending $15,000 to $60,000 a year for college, minimizing the time a student is in college can have significant savings. You can often find in reference books and magazines the percentage of students who graduate after four, five, or six years. That is a good statistic to know, but I think it is also important to know the number of students who graduate on time for their program. For example, almost all engineering students will spend a minimum of five years at a college to get their degree, so knowing how many students graduate in six years does not tell me how many students actually graduated on time in five years. Another good place to find graduation rates is at www.CollegeResults.org, the school's CDS, and www.nces.ed.gov/collegenavigator.

A very low graduation rate can be quite informative, especially since the national averages are extremely low. Obviously if a student stays in college more than four years, the cost of college rises.

Moreover, don't put too much emphasis on high graduation rates. Attending a college with a high graduation rate does not mean that your student will get a good education while at the college.

The Educational Policy Committee, a group that advises the University of North Carolina's Faculty Council on issues dealing with education at UNC Chapel Hill, recently found that an astonishing 82% of the grades issued in fall 2007 to undergrads were As and Bs. That's up from 77% from 2000. They also found that the average undergraduate GPA increased from 2.976 in 1995 to 3.2 in 2007. The committee found that GPAs were rising an average of 0.0185 points per year.

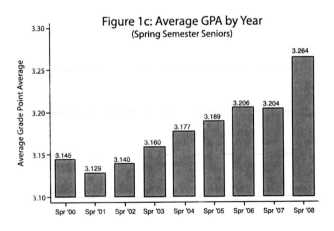

Figure 1c: Average GPA by Year
(Spring Semester Seniors)

Grade inflation might be due to UNC admitting sma
who are more capable and more diligent. But it also might be due ،
fessors that don't want the trouble that comes with giving out a low grade.
The committee chairman, Peter Gordon, believes some of problem with
grade inflation has to do with a Web site called www.myedu.com. This
Web site posts the average grades handed out by specific teachers and
student feedback on these classes. Because professors are partly judged
by student feedback, it could put added pressure on the professors to
inflate grades.

With the majority of students at UNC receiving As and Bs, you would
expect to see high graduation rates. At the University of North Carolina
at Chapel Hill, they have a four year graduation rate of 73%, a five year
graduation rate of 83%, and a six year graduation rate of 86%.

Grade inflation is happening not only at UNC Chapel Hill but also
at colleges and universities all across America. This is not to suggest that
you will not get a good undergraduate degree from UNC but to make a
point about graduation rates. While it is a good fact to look at and
consider, more information is needed to get a better overall picture of
each college or university.

4. Acceptance Rate

With the assistance of the Internet and the common application,
many students apply to a larger number of colleges. It is not uncommon
for colleges to have a 20% increase in their applicant pool over the previous
year. The acceptance rate is a good number to review to see how hard it
is to get into the school, and it might help a family with determining how
motivated the school is to recruit freshmen.

Acceptance rate is a mathematical calculation of the total number of
freshmen accepted divided by the total freshmen who applied to the
college. For example, say a college only accepted 2,000 applicants out of
30,000 that applied; then the acceptance rate is 6.6%. The most popular
colleges usually have very low acceptance rates due to the perceived
academic reputation, name recognition, or sports teams.

In most cases, the lower the acceptance rate, the larger the endowment
and therefore potentially the more money to recruit incoming freshmen.

A high acceptance rate number by itself does not mean a college will necessarily give more aid, but if you look at it in conjunction with the additional facts and figures discussed below, you will start to form a better picture of how strong a college can financially recruit new students. You can calculate the acceptance rate using admissions data from the college's Common Data Set (CDS).

5. Yield Percentage

Yield percentage is similar to the acceptance rate calculation because it helps a parent to decide which schools are competitive and which schools probably have large endowments. The more competitive the college, the higher the yield percentage and more than likely the higher the endowment will be.

To calculate the yield, a college will divide the total number of students who enrolled at the school and divide this number by students accepted at the college. Just as airlines book more passengers than they have seats, colleges accept more students than they need to fill their freshman class. This is essential to the colleges because the colleges know that most students apply to four to six colleges. If a college only accepts 2,000 applications and actually enrolls 1,800 of these students, then the yield would be 90%. A high yield by itself does not mean a family should expect to receive more aid, especially with very competitive colleges. You can calculate the acceptance rate using admissions data from the college's Common Data Set (CDS).

6. Average Merit-based Aid

You can go to www.collegeboard.com to find the average non-need-based aid, but the best source is always the Common Data Set (CDS). Using the CDS, you can see actual numbers and the breakdown between need-based and non-need-based scholarships and grants. You will also be able to see the total amount of tuition waivers, the total amount of state scholarship money given, and even the total amount of private scholarships given by the college. But most importantly you can find the following on the CDS: average dollar amount of institutional non-need-based scholarship and grant aid awarded to students.

This is a very important number when we start to review your financial aid award letters!

As mentioned earlier, colleges determine their own criteria when it comes to deciding which students qualify for merit aid. Some colleges will tell you exactly what SAT score and what GPA you will need to achieve to get a specific amount of aid (e.g., a 3.5 GPA and a 1240 on your SAT to receive an $11,000 University Grant). A good example of this is happening locally is at the University at South Carolina and at Clemson University. To get in-state tuition at the University at South Carolina and at Clemson University for an out-of-state student, the colleges set a minimum SAT score with a minimum GPA that a student must achieve every year.

The majority of colleges will factor in a student's GPA, the difficulty of the student's high school coursework, standardized test scores, and extracurricular activities to determine who receives merit aid. Be careful to use this number only as a baseline to see how well a college can spend money to recruit new students. This is an average number, so some students received far less money than the published "average" merit aid number. Please remember that the colleges will be comparing all the strengths of all the students, and the merit aid will also vary.

7. Percentage of Need Met

If you remember from our earlier discussion, I explained how need-based aid is calculated using the expected family contribution number (EFC) and the cost of attendance (COA):

$$COA - EFC = FINANCIAL\ NEED$$

Colleges are not required or obligated to meet the entire financial need of a family! For example, if the COA at a college is $30,000 and the EFC is $16,000, then the financial need is $14,000. This financial need of $14,000 will usually consist of any combination of the following: family's private scholarship monies, federal grants, state grants, Stafford Loan, Perkins Loan, and federal or college work-study.

It is important to know the average amount of financial need a college may be able to give a family. The percentage of need met is the total amount of aid the college offers to meet in the above formula. Continuing with the above example, say the college only offered $8,000 in assistance to cover the need of $14,000. The ratio created by the $8,000 divided by the $14,000 equals 57% of need met. Even though the family needs $14,000, the college only meets 57% of this need by offering the family $8,000 in aid. The package of assistance will be a combination of federal, state, and college grants and subsidized loans. Some colleges use a term called "Packaging PLUS" to mask the gap between a family's financial need and the amount given by the college by using Unsubsidized Stafford and Parent PLUS Loans, which are loans not based upon need.

PERCENTAGE OF NEED MET = ASSISTANCE
DIVIDED BY THE NEED

Please do not assume that your family will receive the average percentage of need met. Because this is an average number, a family could receive a much lower aid amount or a much higher aid package than the average.

On the College Board Web site, you will find out the average percent of need met, the average need-based loan, and the average need-based scholarship or grants. If you look at the college's CDS, you will find the actual amount given by the college under the line average need-based scholarship or grant award.

If you calculate your EFC and you believe you might receive need-based aid, you will want to know which colleges might meet your need and which colleges will not meet your financial need. Knowing the percentage of need-based aid number will also be important when you review your official financial aid award letter.

8. Retention Rate

If a college has a low retention rate, then you might want to question the college on why students are not coming back to their school. Is it because the neighborhood is changing around the college? Or maybe it is because the hot water does not work in the freshman dorm rooms, or maybe the campus has become unsafe? You can easily find this number on the CDS. You should also compare this to the other colleges so that you have a good baseline of what is considered a good retention rate or a poor retention rate.

9. Gender Acceptance Rate

Contrary to what most of us might think, my male students tend not to apply to colleges with a high number of females because they believe they would feel outnumbered if they attended the school. In addition, some of my female students don't want to apply to colleges that already have a high percentage of female undergraduates because of the perceived competition with other females at the school.

The college administrators know that most boys and girls in America see eye to eye with my students, so they would like to equalize the number of men and women on campus. Women already make up more than 56% of the total number of undergraduates in America, and there are more academically qualified girls applying to college than boys. It is generally harder for a woman with the same college numbers as a man to get in the same college because the colleges are trying to increase the number of males enrolled in order to even the ratio of males to females.

But don't fret, women; while men will have a slight competitive advantage if they apply to a college with more females, women will have a competitive advantage if they apply to schools with a greater percentage of males. It is important to know this if there is already a large male or female population on campus. This will help you identify which colleges will offer a generous financial aid package to either males or females to equalize their student population.

10. Need-blind, Need-aware, and Full-need Colleges

It is important to know if the colleges you are considering are need-blind, need-aware, or full-need colleges because this will have a huge impact on a financial aid package.

Need-blind colleges are colleges that are supposed to accept or deny applicants without considering an applicant's financial situation. Need-aware colleges are schools that rank the applicants on a scale. The most desirable applicants are awarded the best financial aid packages based upon the family's financial need and EFC number. Full-need colleges are colleges in which the school has a financial aid policy that meets the full financial need of all its admitted students. Please be aware that not all need-blind colleges are full-need colleges and that some need-blind colleges become need-aware when selecting students off the wait list.

Once you calculate your EFC number in step 14, you will have a better picture of how this number might affect an award letter. For example, a family calculates their EFC to be $78,000 per year using the FAFSA form. If their son or daughter applies to a full-need elite private college that costs $56,000 a year, then more than likely they will receive very little financial aid from the college because the family has not demonstrated financial need based upon the financial need calculation (cost of attendance minus expected family contribution = financial need).

COA:	$56,000
EFC:	$78,000
FN:	$0

I would suggest this family look for a college that is not full-need but one that recruits students by offering tuition discounts and merit aid.

However, if this same family calculated their EFC to be only $5,000 a year, then a full-need college is a good choice because the college will meet the full demonstrated financial need of $51,000.

COA:	$56,000
EFC:	$5,000
FN:	$51,000

Wikipedia.com lists the colleges that offer both need-blind admissions and full-need for U.S. students (http://en.wikipedia.org/wiki/Need-blind_admission):

1. Beloit College
2. Boston College
3. Bowdoin College
4. Brandeis University
5. Brown University
6. California Institute of Technology
7. Carnegie Mellon University
8. Claremont McKenna College
9. College of the Holy Cross
10. Columbia University
11. Cornell University
12. Cooper Union
13. Davidson College
14. Denison University
15. Duke University
16. Emory University
17. Georgetown University
18. Grinnell College
19. Hamilton College
20. Haverford College
21. Knox College
22. Lawrence University
23. Middlebury College
24. Northwestern University
25. Pomona College
26. Rice University
27. Stanford University
28. Swarthmore College
29. University of Chicago
30. University of Miami
31. University of Notre Dame
32. University of Pennsylvania
33. University of Richmond
34. University of Rochester
35. University of Southern California

36. University of Virginia
37. Vassar College
38. Vanderbilt University
39. Wake Forest University
40. Wellesley College
41. Wesleyan University
42. Williams College

The above factors covered in this chapter are by no means all the facts that you should consider. However, it is a good start to evaluating the schools. This data contributes to the family's overall insight on the college's ability to invest in their incoming freshman class, the college's future goals, and the type of student the college would like to recruit.

CHAPTER 23

STEP 10: Dismissal of Colleges

I f paying for college is a concern and if the high cost of college is causes you anxiety (and for most middle-income families in America, this is their number one concern), then you need to take this very important step. To have the best opportunity to get a great financial aid award letter from these schools, **you need to eliminate all the colleges in which a student is not in the top 25% of SAT or ACT scores.**

Compare the student's college numbers you gathered in **step 7** with the data you just collected on the 25th percentile, median, and 75th percentile SAT and ACT scores of each college.

Where does the student fit compared to the last year's freshman SAT/ACT scores? Is he or she in the 75th percentile, 25th percentile, or near the median? For example, let's use the following numbers as an example of what you might see on a college CDS:

25th Percentile	Median	75th Percentile
1180	1325	1390

If your child scored an 1130 on the SAT (verbal and math), he or she would be in the bottom 25th percentile compared to last year's freshmen. Not only are the chances of the student getting accepted at this college very poor, but the chances that this college will try to recruit this child by giving him or her a great financial aid package are also very small. If the student scored a 1350, the student would still be close to median or average. Again, the college may or may not accept the student, and more than likely they will not offer the family a great financial aid package because the student is average compared to the other entering freshmen. Now, if the student scored 1400, we know that the student will be accepted at the school and more than likely will be offered a good financial aid package if the college has the money to recruit students.

If a student does not have 6 to 10 colleges that meet his or her criteria and in which he or she scored in the 75th percentile on the standardized test, then the student needs to increase the geographic range of colleges to consider or eliminate some other criteria. It is essential to find 6 to 10 colleges that the student would like to attend, but the student must also be in the top 25% scoring on the SAT or ACT.

If a student does not have a high enough SAT or ACT score to be in the top 25% of his or her absolute favorite school, the family should still go through the process of finding 6 to 10 colleges that would still fit the student's criteria. Many times the student will find that these other colleges are great alternatives and will fall in love with one of them.

Moreover, if the student's SAT/ACT score is not quite high enough to be in the 75th percentile of his or her favorite school, it helps the student know how he or she compares to other students and what score he or she needs to get the next time he or she takes the SAT or ACT. This will help motivate students study for the SAT/ACT because they now have a tangible goal to aim for.

Also, please keep in mind what we discussed in the first section of this book when we talked about narrowing down colleges:

1. Having a degree from a so-called "prestigious college" will NOT enhance learning or get you a better job.
2. Not scoring well on the SAT or ACT does NOT mean a start to a less successful future and a less-than-stellar college experience.

If the student *has* to attend a particular college in which he or she is not in the top 25%, plan on the student attending another college for two years while making all As and then transferring to the student's favorite college after his or her sophomore year.

Transfer in Later

Mark Cook was determined to go to Johns Hopkins University. Mark performed well on his SAT, but he did not score high enough to be in the

75th percentile of the freshman class at Johns Hopkins. As a result, Mark was accepted at Johns Hopkins University, but the university did not offer Mark and his family a great financial aid package. The Cook family decided Mark would attend the school anyway even though the family's college savings would be exhausted after one year. Mark spent two years at Johns Hopkins before transferring to a local state school. I asked Mark his main reason for transferring, and he replied, "I felt different than my classmates, and everyone seemed ultra-competitive. I felt out of place." The parents spent all of their college savings during the first year and borrowed money for his second year of college because their savings had been exhausted. Mark did complete his education, but the cost of getting his degree at a local state school was over $135,000! The family paid for the cost of a private college for the first two years when they did not have to do so. As you can see, Mark did not use emotional intelligence or leverage during his college selection, and it cost the family dearly!

I work with families that do the exact opposite of what Mark did. The students attend two years at a state school or community college and then transfer to their preferred college of choice. In general, transfer students do not get as favorable financial aid awards, but the family will still save money overall because the student attended the college of their choice while paying state school prices for the first two years.

Apply to Colleges Outside Your Region

If you still are unable to find at least six colleges in which you are not in the top 75th percentile on the standardized test, you may need to add colleges outside your geographic region. Most individuals separate all the colleges and universities in America into four general regions: Northeast, Southeast, Midwest, and West. To get a listing of which states fall into each region, please go to my Web site at www.collegeaidformiddleclass.com.

By narrowing down colleges that fit the criteria that you decided upon in **step 5,** you probably identified a few colleges that were out-of-state public schools or even private colleges that you believed were too far away from home. If you read the mission statement and the CDS of these schools, you probably found that most colleges put a lot of emphasis on diversity at their school. *This is your trump card* if you are not in the top 75th percentile of SAT or ACT test scores.

Colleges in the West, Midwest, and Northeast have far fewer freshman applicants from the Southeast region and vice versa. Many of these colleges and universities will discount their cost by providing financial assistance to recruit incoming freshmen from a different region. For example, a college in Florida might like to recruit students from the Midwest to enhance its geographic diversity.

By applying only to colleges in which the student is in the top 25% of incoming freshmen (or in the 75th percentile or above), he or she is increasing his or her chances of academic success and happiness. Not only that, but the student also positions himself or herself to be recruited by business and graduate schools upon graduation.

Most importantly, colleges and universities will see a prospective student differently if the student is in the top 25% of incoming freshmen. The colleges will now want to recruit this student and will do what they can to keep this student from attending other competing colleges and universities.

Remember, you will not know if a college wants your child until you receive the financial aid award letter and the type of financial aid that is being offered. Unfortunately you will not receive an official award letter until late spring, so before you apply, you should get the facts about the school and try to determine if the prospective college or university will be able to offer aid to the students that they want to recruit.

Let's go back to the example of the family helping a young female purchase a dress for her prom. The family was able to narrow down the appropriate dresses easily by knowing what to look for in a dress before they entered the dress shop. The family was able to eliminate 99% of the dresses in the shop to around 35 dresses that fit the family's criteria. From the dresses that fit the family's criteria, the family will then eliminate the ones that are not quite the right color or cut, exactly as a family should eliminate all colleges in which the student is not in the 75th percentile of SAT and/or ACT scores.

CHAPTER 24

STEP 11: In "Debth" Study: Is the Movie Critic Always Right?

Life in general is all about making educated guesses on multiple choice tests. There are no clear-cut answers in life. Before we purchase a new car, buy a home, or anything else in life, we usually settle on one item that we like the best and that we believe meets the desires and needs that we have set. We make an educated guess on the final selection that we guess will meet our needs and desires. However, there are always multiple right answers in life and in your college choices.

*Many families wrongly believe that there is **only one college** that would be a perfect fit for their child. In reality, there are **multiple colleges** that will be a good fit, and you need to apply to all of those. But before you know if it will be a good fit, you must become more educated about the schools so you can identify those 6 to 10 colleges that would be a great fit!*

To become an educated consumer, use many sources of information such as the Web, print materials, the colleges' own Web pages, magazines, marketing information from colleges, high school and college counselors, visits to the school, and so on to get a better picture of colleges that would be a good fit and meet your criteria.

Did you see the movie *Transformers: Revenge of the Fallen*? Did you happen to see *The Da Vinci Code,* or *Pirates of the Caribbean: At World's End*? Do you know what these three movies have in common? Most movie critics gave them poor reviews, yet they all had tremendous box office successes. For example, *Transformers: Revenge of the Fallen* grossed over $600 million worldwide!

Think of all the various college rankings publications and other printed material comparing different colleges like movie critics. They are well-respected, knowledgeable, informative, and packed with opinions.

However, the most important opinion is yours and yours alone. Make use of all of the sources of information and blend them to form a solid foundation about the schools.

On the other hand, please recognize that there are apparent limitations on each source. For example, when using the Internet, please make sure you go to the college's own Web site, the College Board Web site, the Department of Education Web site, and the IRS Web site, just to name a few. (Also go to www.collegeaidformiddleclass.com for great resources to use for college selections.) Keep in mind that you can get overwhelmed by the information and that some of the Web sites might not be updated.

With the abundant printed material like *Peterson's Four-Year Colleges, Rugg's Recommendation on Colleges, U.S. News & World Report,* there is a wealth of valuable information, but sometimes the facts seem conflicting. Make sure you realize that the information in these resources sometimes can be at least a year old.

You will want to do more extensive research on the colleges now on your list. You want to become an educated consumer!

Remember the analogy of the girl selecting the perfect prom dress? Just as this family would not let any one single factor determine which dress the daughter would choose, you should not let a single factor like weather, geography, prestige, location, or size determine where your child should attend college. If more than one or two factors or criteria don't fit, then you might want to eliminate the college from your list of consideration.

CHAPTER 25

STEP 12: The L.U.C.K.Y. Visit

"Luck is believing you're lucky."
— Tennessee Williams

The college visit is the most important step to eliminate FEAR and gain emotional intelligence. The college visit will allow a parent and a student to perform hands-on research and fact-finding at the school to formulate their own opinions.

LUCK is sometimes referred to as laboring under correct knowledge. That is a great way to describe the college visit if you have followed all the steps up to this point. If you have not, then you will waste valuable time, resources, and money visiting colleges that are not good fits for your child. You could even be visiting colleges that your child will fall in love with but does not qualify for academically. Even worse, you could be visiting colleges that the child loves, you love, and fits the child perfectly socially and academically, but you will not be able to afford it because you did not research the financial aid numbers before the visit.

In working with families through the years, I have heard numerous stories about how they have visited over 10 colleges and the student really has not liked any of them! I already know why, but I like to ask these families why they picked these colleges to visit? They always tell me basically the same thing: "From our research and from talking with others, we thought these colleges would be a good fit."

These families were not only out of luck, but they were not <u>l</u>aboring <u>u</u>nder <u>c</u>orrect <u>k</u>nowledge. They were blindly visiting colleges based on the opinions of others, without knowing what the student was looking for in a college, without knowing the family's criteria in a good college for the child, and without eliminating FEAR and letting emotional intelligence guide them.

However, if you are LUCKY and have followed my steps, you will visit colleges without FEAR, with emotional intelligence, and with enough facts to be an educated consumer. I like to call this looking at universities and colleges knowing yourself (LUCKY). It's always better to be **LUCKY** *than just good*!

For the college student and parent who have used all the resources to become an educated consumer to help them narrow down the colleges to approximately 10, it is now time for the college visit.

Like I said before, life is a series of multiple choice tests, and there are also multiple correct answers in life. Don't think that there is only one college that would be a good fit for a student. There are always multiple right answers and multiple right colleges for students!

Much like the daughter trying on the dress in the dressing room to get further clarification, the college visit gives the parents and students the opportunity to try out the college.

College visits are extremely important. From working with my clients, I have noticed that many young women can tell if they like a college within 30 minutes of visiting the school. They will step out of the car, look around, and say either, "Oh, I like this" or "Nope, let's go back home!" I cannot tell you why women have this ability, but it is like they have another sense that we men do not have. (To learn what questions to ask and what you should look at during the college visit, please visit my Web site www.collegeaidformiddleclass.com.) Sometimes it takes a little longer for a young man, but he will know, as well, if the college is a good fit.

The college visits will verify if your research is correct, and it will help further narrow your college choices down to your final 6 to 10 colleges just like the young lady who was able to walk out of the dressing room with 6 to 10 prom dresses that she would be glad to wear.

I have to warn you that the college visits might also change your mind on the criteria that you selected in **step 5**. It actually happens quite often that a child will change his or her mind. For example, a student might think initially that he or she would like to attend a large state college, so the family narrows down the colleges based on attending a large state school and many more criteria. They then continue to **step 8** and reduce the colleges from 40 down to 6 to 10 colleges. The family now decides to visit the six colleges that they think the student would like to attend, and after visiting the large campuses, the student thinks that the large state school is just too big! This is okay, because it is better to find out now than after a student enrolls. The family will need to start back at **step 5** and look for colleges with the same criteria except with a smaller student population. I used student population for this example, but we could substitute this with any other criteria.

It is always better to try to visit a college while the college is in session. You get a better feel for the atmosphere on campus, and you have the opportunity to speak with the students. However, I know a lot of my parents and students only have time to visit on summer break or during the holidays. That's okay too; I would still suggest you visit even if you cannot make it while the classes are in session.

College Visitation Checklist

The main objective of the college visit is to confirm that it meets the criteria that you have previously decided on. A college might have a great Web site, it might look like the perfect fit on paper, but you will not know until you set foot on campus. You will find out if the college's "personality" fits with the personality of the student by seeing firsthand the college's programs, policies, and social setting. Only during this visit can the student experience this. Following is a checklist of things to do to ensure a productive college visitation.

1. Make visitation arrangements on the college's Web site. You will find a schedule of tours or information sessions. You will also find driving directions and maybe even a list of nearby hotels. If possible, try scheduling the visit on a weekday during the school term.
    a. Friday is good because you can see the academic side in the morning and the weekend side in the evening.
    b. Scheduling a tour around 10:00 a.m. works well because you will complete the tour around lunchtime. Some schools will invite you to eat in the cafeteria. This is a good opportunity to try the food and speak with other students.

2. While on campus, you should ask strategic questions of the following:
    a. Admissions office
    b. Financial aid office
    c. Career placement office
    d. Faculty
    e. Athletic department
    f. Students

3. Some questions you may ask of administrators of the school are:
    a. What percentage of students graduate in four, five, and six years?
    b. What is your freshman retention rate or transfer rate?
    c. What was the average tuition increase over the past five years?
    d. Do you have a career placement center office, and what services does it provide? Can alumni use it?

4. Some questions to ask students currently enrolled at the school are:
    a. What do you like most about this college and why did you decided to attend this college?
    b. What is the worst aspect of this school?
    c. Do graduate students or professors teach introductory classes?
    d. How accessible are professors outside of class?

5. Sit in on a class or speak with a professor in the department your student is thinking about majoring in.

6. College interview: This is a great time to do a college interview. It is an opportunity to show interest in the college. Make sure you have a topic in mind that you can talk about for 15 minutes before you go. Arrive early to make sure you are on time.

7. Ask if you can stay overnight in a dorm. This is the best way to see what college life is really like.

8. See more than the "statue and new building tour." The tour guide will show you the new buildings and the statues on your official visit. You will hear all the good things about the college. Make sure you walk around on your own so you can speak with other students.

9. Try not to visit more than two schools in one day. You can see more colleges in one day, but I would not recommend it. It is much better to take your time so you are not tired or stressed and so you have time to record your thoughts regarding the visit.

10. Record your thoughts: This is going to be your student's home away from home, so you will need to have a way to record your impressions. More importantly, you need a way to rank the college on how it meets your criteria. Make sure you use the same ranking system or the same systematic way of making notes about your visits everywhere you go. If you don't make good notes or record your thoughts, you will find it difficult to remember what you liked and did not like at each school after visiting numerous colleges. You can find a sample of this at www.collegeaidfor middleclass.com.

11. If you cannot visit the colleges in which you are interested, you should ask the counselor to help you find a video or virtual tour of the campus.

12. Attend college fairs and speak with admissions representatives. Speak with alumni in your area.

13. Based on your evaluation of the responses, rank the colleges.

By collecting facts about the schools and gauging the college's ability to recruit and invest in their incoming freshman class, a family can make an educated, rational decision on their college selection. By combining emotional intelligence, facts, and college visits, you will succeed in your college selection process.

CHAPTER 26

STEP 13: Apply Early to 6 to 10 Colleges

Jennifer's parents drove over an hour and a half from Columbia, SC, to meet with me. Jennifer wanted to study premed in college. She was a very smart young lady who scored 2190 on her SAT. The father was a small business owner with an income of $110,000 a year. They had $160,000 in taxable investments and $150,000 in home equity. There were four members of her family, but Jennifer was the first to go to college. I calculated the family's expected family contribution initially as $34,000, and I was able to show them how to reduce their EFC number to $29,000.

At our very first meetings, Jennifer had her heart set on attending one university, and she did not want to consider any other schools. I had to explain to Jennifer that there are other wonderful colleges and universities that are perfect fits for her that she does not know exist.

I also explained to the family that colleges know who they are competing against for the student. They know this because the financial aid officer can look on the back of the financial aid forms to see the other colleges or universities that receive the each student's forms.

I told her that the colleges and universities are just like you and me. They like to see their money grow, and they do not like to give it away if they do not have to. I explained that we have to encourage the colleges to give you money by making them recruit you. We do this by applying to 6 to 10 colleges, public and private, that you would like to attend.

I told Jennifer that we have to find at least six schools that she would like to attend. She was asked to select two or three colleges she really liked and then add two or three more that she could see herself attending.

Out of the minimum of six colleges, a child will more than likely not be accepted to all of them. If your child applies to only six, he or she might only be accepted at four, and if he or she originally applies to 10, he or she might only get accepted at six colleges.

You need options! Whether you are negotiating a new job offer, a new car purchase, or even a college award letter, you have to be able to walk away from the table if the deal is not right. The more options you have, the better.

I asked Jennifer, "If you apply to only two colleges and you only get accepted at one college, do you think the college will need to offer any money to recruit you? On the other hand, what if you were accepted at six colleges? Do you think the colleges would now have more incentive to offer you money to recruit you?"

Colleges and universities compete athletically as well as academically. These schools know whom they are competing against if the student they are trying to recruit is a good student.

Jennifer then asked me, "If I need more options, why don't I apply to 20 colleges instead of a maximum of 10 schools?"

I replied, "Let's say you applied to the following colleges: Harvard, University of Hawaii, University of North Carolina at Pembroke, Catholic University, and Central Piedmont Community College. When the financial aid officer or the enrollment manager at the schools looks at your financial aid forms to see what other colleges they are competing against, what do you think they will say to themselves?"

Jennifer replied, "That the student I have no idea what I want to do or I have no focus."

I said, "Exactly! It almost looks like you are a fisherman, and you are hoping for any fish (or school) to come by and catch the bait. You need to apply to 6 to 10 colleges that fit you socially and academically and that you would like to attend. This list of schools you apply to needs to be a combination of in-state public schools and private colleges or universities. The public schools need to know that they are competing against the private schools and vice versa. Not all colleges and universities that you apply to will be looking for a white female from South Carolina this year to attend their school. But if we do this the right way, a few of the colleges will be looking for someone just like you! These colleges will not want you to go to a rival institution, so they will want to recruit you. When they recruit you, they will offer you money. You now have options."

We were able to help Jennifer identify 10 colleges that she really liked. She applied to all 10, and we helped the family to reduce their EFC number legally and ethically. By making the colleges compete and by positioning the family's finances correctly, Jennifer was awarded the Carolina Scholarship from the University of North Carolina at Chapel Hill worth $15,000 a year. She also received $2,625 of a Stafford Loan.

Received:	$15,000	Carolina Scholarship
	$ 2,625	Stafford Loan
	$17,625	total aid

At the time, the cost of attendance for an out-of-state student at UNC was $33,477.

- $15,852/year out of pocket to go to an out-of-state, public, tier 1 college ($33,477/year COA)

- Total savings over four years: $73,908

Because of the savings, Jennifer's father said he would be able to retire two years earlier than planned!

CHAPTER 27

STEP 14: Calculate Your EFC Using the FAFSA and CSS Profile Forms

Do not wait until you complete the financial aid forms to determine your expected family contribution. The EFC is a number that is calculated by the government and the colleges to determine how much money you can contribute towards college. You need to know in advance if you are able to qualify for need-based aid, so it is imperative that you find out what your EFC number is today. To calculate your EFC, you need to begin by plugging in your numbers using the Free Application for Federal Student Aid (FAFSA) and the CSS Financial Aid Profile formulas.

Some colleges use the Federal Methodology (FM) to determine your EFC number. Most all public colleges use the FM. All four-year colleges that give out federal need-based aid use the FM and the FAFSA to arrive at this number. The FAFSA will look at your family size, age of the older parent, parent and student assets, parent and student taxable and non-taxable income, taxes paid, and the student's dependency status. The FM does not consider the net value of your home, but it will consider second homes or other real estate values.

To calculate your EFC using the FAFSA, you can go to www.FSFSA4 caster.ed.gov. The government uses the FAFSA to determine if you are eligible to receive federal money such as the Pell Grant, the Supplemental Educational Opportunity Grant, and the Stafford Loans.

The CSS Profile form uses the same basic information as the FAFSA. But it goes much deeper and is more detailed. Approximately 250 colleges use the CSS Profile form, as well as the FAFSA form, to calculate your EFC number. A good place to start to calculate your EFC number using the profile form is www.FinAid.org.

Most all good college planners will also calculate your EFC number using the FAFSA and the CSS Profile form so you will know where you stand. There are ways you can legally and ethically reduce your EFC number to potentially qualify for more financial aid. You can take control of this number.

CHAPTER 28

STEP 15: Cash Flow Is King:
Financial Leaks and Opportunity Cost

Increasing cash flow during the college years is essential to helping parents pay for or save for college. Most parents want to know how they can achieve higher rates of return on their college savings investments. Most parents want to know where they can get products that achieve higher rates of return and superior performance on their current college savings investment, which can lead to more risks. *Risk is something that you want to avoid with college savings money while your child is in high school and in college.*

Parents need to realize that they can lose money unknowingly. Since expenses will go up considerably while a child is in college, focusing on avoiding unnecessary fees and expenses is essential to a good plan to pay for college. Parents will multiply their returns and increase cash flow if they concentrate on eliminating these fees and avoiding areas that erode their college savings.

By recapturing these unnecessary charges and costs, parents now have more cash flow during the college years to invest and pay back the student's college loans after the student graduates. The best part about eliminating these preventable expenditures is that parents will usually not have to change their current lifestyle to avoid them. *Financial leaks* are any area in a parent's overall financial plan in which they are unintentionally losing money through unnecessary charges and expenses.

By eliminating these areas of inefficiencies, parents who have no college savings now have one of the biggest opportunities to start saving immediately by freeing up money that they did not think they had. The best possibility to recapture these financial leaks usually fall in one of the below areas:

1. Secured and unsecured debt
2. Taxes
3. Insurance (auto, home, life, etc.)
4. Investment costs

The definition of *opportunity costs* is the benefits you could have received by taking an alternative action. Most families believe that their child should not go to work full time until after he or she graduates from college. Families know that the opportunity cost of four years of lost wages is worth it because the child's degree will enable him or her to receive much higher salaries over the student's lifetime to offset those lost wages.

For example, a family is losing $10 a month unknowingly because of an avoidable fee. The family currently has some money invested for college with a 5% return. In this example, the family is losing $10 a month, or $120 a year. The opportunity cost is not only the $10 a month, but the 5% rate of return that this $10 would have made if they could have invested the $10 into their college investing account. Moreover, this family also loses the interest compounding on this money in the account as well. The first month the opportunity cost would be $10.50 because the family lost not only the $10 to invest but also the 5% rate of return this money could have earned for the family. In the second month, the opportunity cost increases because the family again lost the $10 to an avoidable fee. More importantly, the opportunity cost increases to $21.53 because the family not only lost the $20 but also lost the ability for the second month's lost fee of $10 to be invested at 5% and the first month's $10.50 to be invested at 5% for one month.

Month	Financial Leak	5% Return	Opportunity Cost
1	$10	$10.50	$10.50
2	$10	$11.03	$21.03
3	$10	$12.10	$32.10
4	$10	$13.78	$43.78
5	$10	$16.15	$56.15
6	$10	$19.33	$69.33

Month	Financial Leak	5% Return	Opportunity Cost
7	$10	$23.48	$83.48
8	$10	$28.79	$98.79
9	$10	$35.55	$115.55
10	$10	$44.09	$134.09
11	$10	$54.83	$154.83
12	$10	$68.31	$178.31

This family's opportunity cost is not $120 a year but *$178.31* because of a financial leak of just $10 a month. As you can see, having a small financial leak of just $10 a month can have a huge impact.

This is why I like to use the term financial leak to describe what is happening to most American families. Let's use the example of pouring water into a cup. If that cup has holes in the side, it does not matter how much water we pour into the cup, because it will never be filled. Think of the water as families trying to get higher rates of return and save more money to fill their financial cup. Until we plug these financial leaks, we will never have enough money to achieve our goals. But if we plug the holes first, it does not matter if we pour in a lot of water at one time or contribute small drops over several years; every drop will go toward filling the cup.

Let's use another example of trying to keep a small boat afloat in the water. If we have a boat that has many leaks, it is almost impossible to keep it afloat no matter how hard we work to bail out the water. The boat will eventually sink. Some people will suggest that this boat owner just needs more manpower to bail more water because they believe that putting more resources on the problem will help. Some people will suggest that the boat owner use a bigger bucket to bail the water out faster because getting a better rate of return will keep the boat afloat. However, if the boat owner would just patch the leaks in the boat to begin with, the boat owner wouldn't need more resources or better rates of return to keep the boat afloat. Just one person with the leaks plugged can keep the boat afloat and on course to his or her financial objectives.

Fixing the Personal Tax Leak

The aid strategies that I will discuss are complicated. Because every family's financial picture is different, I can in no way cover every scenario or give specific advice. Moreover, the strategies below are about increasing cash flow, not about getting financial aid, so these strategies might not be appropriate for every family. While these strategies may or may not help a family reduce their expected family contribution and/or reduce their "ability to pay," they can be used to free up extra cash. It is important to work with a college planner or coach to review the pros and cons to determine if any of these strategies are appropriate.

Much like the unfair college financial aid system, our tax system is also unfair. Our tax laws are not fair because certain tax laws benefit certain individuals or groups. I believe in paying my fair share of taxes because I think of it as a necessary cost of living in the greatest country in the world! Our government needs our taxes to pay for the roads, policemen, firemen, schools, defense, etc. But I think it is every person's right and duty to legally and ethically reduce his or her tax burden.

Robert Kiyosaki, in his *Rich Dad* series of books, does a great job of describing the difference between tax evasion and tax avoidance. He writes that doing something purely to avoid taxes is considered tax evasion. But if you do something with the intent to make more money by starting a business, have better legal security, or increase your cash flow and you happen to reduce your taxes at the same time, then you are avoiding taxes. Avoiding taxes is legal but evading taxes is not!

Below is a chart showing the top U.S. federal marginal income tax rates from 1913 to 2010.

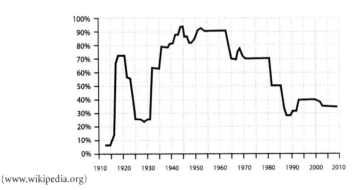

(www.wikipedia.org)

We have had fairly low income taxes over the last few years, and I predict that that is going to change in the near future. When you pay a dollar to the government in taxes that you could have avoided (not evaded), you lose what the dollar could have earned for you if you had invested it, and you lose the compound interest the dollar could have earned for you as well. That lost dollar and lost interest is the opportunity cost of paying an unnecessary tax and a financial leak that needs to be fixed.

This advice is not about skirting the system or lying about your finances to deceive anyone. This general advice is about legally and ethically emboldening families to maximize their financial aid offers and minimize their cost of college by providing tactics and strategies for families to get the aid that they deserve.

If you go to a bank to try to get a loan, you want to show the bank the best financial picture as possible. On the other hand, when you complete the financial aid forms, you want to show them the worst financial picture as possible.

The financial aid forms and your federal taxes are combined at the hip. They are linked together. The financial aid forms will ask you what you made from January 1st of your student's junior year to December 31st of your student's senior year. This is called your base year, and it is very important.

There are many different strategies to reduce your income. For example, becoming an independent contractor is a great way for some parents who are not business owners.

Independent Contractor

If you are a W-2 employee and you have unreimbursed business expenses, you may become an independent contractor. While salaried employees are allowed to take an itemized tax deduction for these unreimbursed business expenses, it does not lower the family's income on the financial aid forms. By becoming an independent contractor, you can deduct the business expenses and lower your adjusted gross income. You will need to meet the IRS guidelines of a qualified independent contractor and consult your accountant to see if the advantages outweigh the disadvantages.

If you are a high-income earner or business owner and you know you will not qualify for financial aid, there are many unique strategies you can implement to reduce the cost of college by finding these tax leakages. These cash flow and income shifting strategies can be an effective tax reduction tactic to improve a family's cash flow. Below are a few of the strategies you might want to consider:

Assets in Your Child's Name

If you think you qualify for financial aid, **do not** put assets in the child's name. Even if your EFC numbers look high, you should not assume that you will not qualify for aid. Work with a qualified advisor to see if the below strategies are appropriate.

Hire Your Child

By transferring income from the parent's high tax bracket to the child's lower tax bracket, a parent's tax burden can be reduced. In 2010, the child's first $5,700 of earned income is taxed at zero and the next $8,350 of earned income is taxed at just 10%. Among other things, a child can be employed to: (1) help move, (2) keep track of investments, (3) help with home office work, or (4) perform household duties. In addition to the tax savings benefit of hiring a child, the child is now eligible to contribute to a retirement account since they now have earned income. The family can now use the retirement account as a college savings account. The Roth IRA may be the best type to use because the contributions may be withdrawn tax free and penalty free for college expenses.

Gift or Sale and Lease Back

Have you ever thought about gifting a fully depreciated property or equipment to your child through your business? Well, this is another great way of income-shifting! You can gift or sale and lease back anything, including cars, equipment, or even a warehouse.

Education Reimbursement Plan (IRC Sec. 127)

When I went back to college to get my MBA, General Electric Plastics paid for my college costs through their tuition reimbursement plan. GE was able to write this off as a business expense, and I was able to use this money to pay for college. Not only can large corporations do this, but business owners can as well. An employer may reimburse an employee/ child for job-related education courses. The reimbursement is a tax deduction for the business. Business owners can deduct up to $5,250 per year for two years as a business deduction. The business owner will need to employ his or her child and must use specific forms and guidelines to qualify.

Using Fringe Benefits

If you employ your child, you might be able to deduct his or her car as an expense. A company car can be considered a working condition fringe benefit. If the car qualifies as a working condition fringe benefit, then 100% of the value of that business use is exempted from the child's (employee's) income. If, however, the personal use of a company car is included in the child's (employee's) income, **the business can recover the entire cost of the company car as if it were used entirely for business purposes!** In addition, the use of a computer and cell phones can be considered a fringe benefit as well. The business receives a tax deduction for these expenses, and the child would report the value of the personal use as a taxable fringe benefit.

Gift of Appreciated Assets

This is a pretty simple concept that can have huge tax savings. A business owner or high-income earner parent with a larger tax bracket can gift appreciated assets to a child in a lower tax bracket. By shifting the appreciated asset from the high tax bracket to a lower tax bracket, you can reduce the family's taxes and increase cash flow when the child sells the asset.

Shifting After-tax Dollars to Child

After-tax dollars are accounts on which the parents have already paid taxes. These are non-retirement accounts. Parents that don't have any appreciated assets or own a business still have opportunities to increase their family's cash flow. These parents can shift any after-tax dollars to the child through annual gifts as early as possible. By gifting the investments to the child early, the family is able to save their taxes because now any growth and earnings on the investment are taxed at the child's rate and not the parents' higher tax rate. Many parents use custodial accounts to shift assets to a child. The accounts are fairly simple to establish, and parents are able to keep control of the assets until the child is 18 or 21 years of age.

Business Entity

You can also shift income to a child by forming an S corporation, a limited liability company (LLC), and/or a family partnership. One question I'm asked most frequently is, "Which business entity is right for my family?" You should always seek proper tax and legal advice before making that decision because each business entity has its advantages and disadvantages. However, they are all great ways to shift income to a child while parents maintain control of the assets.

Case study: The Willis family had a daughter that was a rising sophomore in college. The daughter wanted to live in off-campus housing with two of her friends for the final few years of college. The Willises were astonished at how expensive a dorm room was, so they thought this might be a good idea. After some careful planning with me, they decided to purchase a three bedroom, two and a half bath house close to campus using $30,000 of HELOC equity line of credit from their primary home. With the help of a local attorney, they formed a limited liability company and were able to structure the loan so that the corporation owned the property. The parents were the owners of the corporation, and they hired their daughter to manage the property. The daughter rented the two rooms of the house to her friends at school. The corporation in turn paid the Willises' daughter for managing the property and other expenses for upkeep of the property. This resulted in no taxes on the rental income, and the daughter was able to use the wages to pay some of her education fees and lower her tuition bill considerably. The daughter only needed to take a portion of the Unsubsidized Stafford Loan to cover the remaining tuition. When the Willises' daughter graduated from college, they decided to sell the house for a modest profit. The family was able to pay off the $30,000 HELOC that was used to make the original down payment and the student loan that was in the daughter's name. When you add together the tax savings, the rental payments, and the small profit from the property, the cost of college was almost nothing. Better yet, since the parents paid off the Stafford educational loans that were in the daughter's name, the daughter graduated from college with a good credit score and no student loans!

These are just a few of the ways parents maximize their child's tax capacity to increase cash flow and fix the tax leak. The advantages and disadvantages of the strategies and investments used to shift assets to a child needs to be considered by a qualified advisor or coach.

My recommendation is to work with a certified college planner or a CPA who is knowledgeable about the specific strategies you can use to legally and ethically reduce you income or to find ways to increase cash flow with these unique tax strategies. Remember, these are just a few of the strategies that are available. Working with the right college coach and/or planner can greatly maximize your ability to increase your financial aid package.

Fixing the Debt Leak

There are two basic types of debt: *secured* and *unsecured*. *Secured debt* is a debt with collateral attached to it, such as your home mortgage or car loan. In the event that the borrower cannot pay back the loan, the creditor has the right to take possession of the asset used as collateral. The lender can sell the collateralized asset to recoup the loan amount. Credit cards, personal loans, and medical bills are considered unsecured debt because there is no collateral attached to the debt. *All families should start by eliminating any unsecured debt first because they usually have the highest interest rates.*

I personally love my credit cards. They help me keep track of my expenses and sometimes give me rewards for using them. The credit card companies would not be in business if every family paid their credit card balance off every month. It is a good bet on their part, because it is very easy for a family to take on excessive credit card debt, and many families that I work with do have high debt amounts. These families have a large leak in their financial ship because of the high interest associated with the credit cards. With interest as high as 16% or more, any investment alternatives that offset this high interest are extremely rare. You could image the large opportunity cost! This is a leak that needs to be fixed fast!

How do you fix this financial leak of unsecured problems? We have two options: the *short-term solution* and the *long-term solution.*

The *long-term solution* should only be used if a family has time to eliminate all their unsecured debt before their child enters college. You start by listing all of your unsecured debt:

Credit Card #1: _____Min. Monthly Payment: $ _____
Balance: $_____ APR:_____%

Credit Card #2: _____Min. Monthly Payment: $ _____
Balance: $_____ APR:_____%

Credit Card #3: _____Min. Monthly Payment: $ _____
Balance: $_____ APR:_____%

Personal Loan: _____Min. Monthly Payment: $ _____
Balance: $_____ APR:_____%

Medical Loan: _____Min. Monthly Payment: $ _____
Balance: $_____ APR:_____%

Next, use only the credit card with the lowest interest rate for all of your expenses each month and continue to make the minimum payments to the other unsecured debt. Use any extra cash or money recaptured through financial leakage to pay off the unsecured debt with the highest interest rate. For example, let's say a family has just paid off their highest interest credit card. They no longer are paying the $150 toward this credit card. The family will not pick the next credit card with the highest interest rate. They pick a card that they were making the minimum payment of $50 dollars. The family's new monthly payment toward this card will be $150 plus the $50 for a total payment of $200 a month. The family will need to continue to do this until all the unsecured debt is paid off.

Families that are successful using this method are very meticulous to make sure their spending does not increase during this time frame. It is imperative that their spending habits change so that when all their unsecured debt is paid off, they do not find themselves back in debt.

The *short-term method* is used by the majority of my clients. They need cash flow relief immediately because they have a child going to college in a year or two. This method involves paying off all secured and unsecured debt at one time by transferring the debt to a second mortgage or a home equity loan. *In most cases, a family will realize increases in cash flow, elimination of debt with high interest rates, potential tax savings, and a plan to pay for college.* **Moreover, you can also reduce your EFC number and ability to pay number on the CSS Profile form.**

Case study: The Moore family has two children. One is a sophomore in college, which the parents are paying for with a PLUS Loan. Their second child is attending a private high school that costs $7,000 a year. Their home was once worth over $400,000 but now is worth only $350,000. They owe $149,000 on a 10 year mortgage with a monthly payment of $2,134 at 4.375%. They also have a $78,000 line of credit at 3.5% on a six year fixed loan with a payment of $1,100 a month. Their monthly debt payment is as follows:

Name	Monthly Payment	Debt
1st mortgage	$2,134	$149,000
2nd mortgage	$1,100	$78,000
College	$1,200	*0
Total	$4,434	$227,000
*Used investment account to pay off PLUS Loan		

This family owns a small business, and they have to lay off employees to keep afloat. Cash flow is tight, and their son is going to be joining his sister in college in about 12 months.

We decided to use the money in their current brokerage account to pay off their Parent PLUS Loan. They liked the idea of giving their children some accountability, so we decided to take out loans in the children's name and help them pay off their loans when they graduated from college. We estimated that we would need around $26,000 in two years to pay off the rest of their daughter's loans when she graduates. We also estimated the family would need $75,000 to pay off their son's college loan in five to six years for an in-state school.

We decided to refinance their current home, pay off the remaining balance of their second mortgage, and take $51,000 in cash from their home to help pay off the children's college costs and hopefully their home. Their new loan was for $280,000 on 30 year mortgage at a 5.5% rate with a new monthly debt payment of $1,906 including taxes and interest.

Old Monthly Budget:	$4,434 (all debt)
New Monthly Budget:	$1,906 (mortgage)
Extra Cash Flow:	$2,528

With this extra monthly cash flow of $2,528, we decided to invest $1,200 a month into a college savings account plus the $51,000 of cash we took out of the house when they refinanced.

New Budget:	$1,906
- College Savings:	$1,200
Total Final Budget:	$3,106

Old Monthly Budget:	$4,434
- New Monthly Budget:	$3,106
Extra Cash Flow:	$1,328

As you can see, this still leaves the family with an extra $1,328 a month that they are using as extra cash flow to support their current standard of living. Moreover, when their son graduates from high school, they will no longer have the $7,000 a year private school cost, so they we will use this additional money to cover any miscellaneous college expenses for both children throughout the next few years.

Additionally, by investing $50,000 plus $1,200 a month in an asset that we estimate will average a return of 8% over the next 20 years, the family will be able to pay off *$26,000 of a student loan in three years, $75,000 of a student loan in six years, and pay off their house in 14 years, all while increasing their cash flow*! Moreover, because the family will be paying mostly interest for the first few years on their new 30 year home loan, the family should be able to save tens of thousands of dollars in taxes as well over the life of the loan. Most importantly, the account in which they are saving this money is protected from market risk and is liquid at all times.

If they have the ability to put more money into the savings account in the future due to business growth, the Moore family can decrease the number of years to pay off their house, use the extra money for a wedding, or keep it for retirement.

Fixing the Investment and Insurance Leak

When I review a family's present financial position, I get a feel for where they are today, and I see if they have a plan to pay for college. One area that I sometimes find leakage is in insurance and investment costs.

I am as guilty as anybody. I do not regularly compare insurance rates for my auto, home, disability, and medical insurance. Just the other day, I worked with a family that has not changed insurance carriers for their home and auto insurance in over 15 years. They had not even reviewed their policies with their agent in over six years. I asked them to do me a favor and call their agent, who represented many different insurance carriers, to get a new quote. I advised them to get quotes not only from different carriers to compare prices but also with different deductibles. The family decided to go with a different carrier and increased their car and home insurance deductible from $250 to $500 because they had sufficient income to cover this deductible. By making these changes, the family saved over $1,100 dollar a year that they were able to invest towards their child's college savings plan that we developed together. The opportunity cost of losing $1,100 dollars by not reviewing their insurance plans was astronomical! Without them reviewing their policy, they could have lost the opportunity to have this money invested for their entire lives.

Families should get in the habit of reviewing their investments at least annually to find any hidden costs or fees. These financial leaks can easily be converted to cash flow that can be used for college. One of the best ways to review the performance of an investment is calculating the investment's internal rate of return (IRR). Since you get quarterly and annual performance reports on your mutual fund holdings already, calculating the IRR works best on stock portfolios and brokerage accounts. The IRR is a calculation that shows a family the interest rate or yield percentage at which an investment begins to make more money than it cost to own the investment. Here is a simple example of how to calculate IRR:

You purchase a stock at the beginning of the year for $100, and it pays a dividend at the end of the year of $10. You then sell the stock for $95. To calculate the IRR of the stock, you need to calculate any profit:

Profit = $10 dividend - $5 loss in stock value
Profit = $5
IRR = Profit / Initial Investment
IRR = $5 / $100 = 5%

You can compare the 5% IRR to the other similar investments, the market as a whole, or to an index to get a better idea of how the stock is performing. Remember, hidden cost and fees erode returns.

CHAPTER 29

STEP 16: Asset Planning

A sset planning and positioning is of the *utmost importance in the game of college planning.* It is essential to a family's success in this game. As mentioned before, this advice is not about skirting the financial aid system or lying about your finances to deceive anyone. This general advice is about legally avoiding all assessments on any assets that are held in the student's or the parent's name. With most colleges using enrollment management practices such as collecting geodemographic data, credit ratings on the parents, and rankings of every high school in the United States (to name just a few), the scale is weighted heavily towards college. Asset repositioning will save families thousands of dollars every year that they have a student in college.

Step 16a: Know what assets are assessed on the Federal Methodology (FM), or FAFSA form, and Institutional Methodology (IM), or CSS Profile form.

Student assets: Assessed assets are any cash, money market accounts, CDs, checking, savings, stocks, bonds, mutual funds, mortgages, land, current market value of real estate other than your home, ownership interest in a business, farms, Uniform Gift to Minors Act account (UGMA), Uniform Transfer to Minors Act account (UTMA), student-owned Coverdell Savings Accounts1, and student-owned 529 plans2.

1. Coverdell Savings Account: On the FM, if the student is considered to be an independent student, then the account will be a student asset if the student is age 18 years or older and elected to keep the parent as owner. It will be assessed at 20%.

2. 529: Student-owned 529 plans are student assets on both the FM and IM. 529 plans owned by the student, with the student as the beneficiary, are reported as a parent's asset. A 529 plan owned by the parent, with the student as the beneficiary, is reported as a parent's asset. A 529 plan owned by the parent, with the student's siblings as the beneficiary, is also reported as a parent's asset. An independent student who owns a 529 plan, with the student as the beneficiary, will list it as a student's asset.

529 plans owned by other family members should not be reported on the FM, but colleges will probably ask you to report it on the IM. Even if you do not have to report it, colleges can decide to assess the value and/or distributions as they please. All colleges add the distribution from a 529 plan as untaxed income that are not reported as an asset on the FAFSA and can reduce non-federal aid dollar for dollar.

Student assets are assessed by the colleges at the rate of 20% on the FM and 25% on the IM. For example, if your child has $7,000 in CDs, this will cost $1,400 (FM) to $1,750 (IM) in financial aid every year. Not only will the college assess the student's assets at a high rate, but any of these assets that generate interest income will be assessed at 50 cents out of every dollar earned.

Parent assets: Examples include the following: home (IM)[1], other land and real estate, trust funds, UGMA and UTMA accounts, money market funds, certificates of deposit, stocks, stock options, bonds, other securities, installment and land sales contracts, commodities, mortgages held, parent-owned Coverdell Savings Accounts, parent-owned 529 plans, business2, and farm3.

1. Home: Under the FM, your home or primary residence is not considered part of your assets. However, under the IM, your home will more than likely be included as an asset in the calculation. Some colleges will cap the home value at 2.4 times the parents' income. There are also 28 colleges that cap the amount of home equity to 1.2 times the parents' income. All other rental

property or vacation homes will be counted by both the FM and IM as other real estate.

2. Business: On the FM, you do not include the value of the business if you control over 50% and the business has 100 or fewer employees.

3. Farms: Do not include the value of the farm if you live on and operate the farm. If you do not live on the farm and you own it, you will need to include the value.

Step 16b: Don't be fooled by the asset protection allowance (APA).

Unlike students, who have no asset protection allowance, parents do have this allowance on the FAFSA form. Essentially the APA is the amount of assets that a parent can own for which they will not be penalized. On the FAFSA, the APA is dependent on whether a household has one or two parents and the age of the oldest parent. This can be found at http://studentaid.ed.gov on the tools and resources page under the publications section (titled "Expected Family Contribution Formula").

Starting in 2010-2011, the IM will no longer contain an asset protection allowance but will contain three new allowances: the emergency reserve allowance, the cumulative education savings allowance, and the low-income asset allowance. All of these allowances are added together, and this number is subtracted from the parents' assets (assets minus all debts) to arrive at the total assessed parental assets. For the year 2010-2011, the first $34,450 of the parents' net assets will be assessed at 3%. The assessed rate increases to 4% from the range of $34,450 to $68,900 in assets. Any assets above $68,900 will assessed at a rate of 5%.

The emergency reserve allowance for 2010-2011 will be $20,330 for a family of two, $24,560 for a family of three, $28,230 for four, $31,620 for five, and $34,450 for six. An additional $2,830 will be credited to the family for each additional child with more than six family members.

The annual education savings allowance is a credit given to families saving money for younger siblings to go to college. To calculate this allowance, the profile processor will multiply the parents' income times 1.52% with the maximum number of $2,770. The program will then multiply this number by the number of children not in college (not including the student applicant). The minimum education savings allowance in 2010-2011 is $23,130.

Finally, the low-income asset allowance is fairly self-explanatory. For parents with negative income using the IM calculation, the credited allowance will be equal to the negative income number that was calculated.

Most parents believe that they will not be penalized if they shield assets above the asset protection allowance (APA) and shield assets above the protection allowance on the IM formula. After all, that's what the allowance is for—to protect assets held by the parents and not have them count toward the family's EFC number. For example, in 2010-2011 the APA for a two parent household with the oldest parent being 45 years old would have an APA of $45,500. If this family has $45,000 in assets, normally most people would recommend not shielding the money because the APA is $45,000 and will not be assessed on the FAFSA form.

This is the wrong advice. While I do agree with the concept of shielding the assets, I don't agree with showing the colleges that the family still has $45,000 available to pay their college cost.

The financial aid officer (FAO) reviews these financial aid forms, and it is not in their job description to reduce tuition cost. In fact, it is their job to increase net tuition revenue for the college. They have the latitude to change your EFC number up or down. They will also determine who will receive the college's own money that they use to recruit new students. It is up to the FAO's discretion to increase or reduce your aid package. It is a fact that some colleges will use "your ability to pay" as a factor with merit aid money and tuition discounts. The FAO can clearly see that a family has $45,000 in cash to pay the college's tuition if it is listed on the financial aid forms, even though the $45,000 might be below the family's asset allowance. This $45,000 could come into play when the FAO decides who receives the college's aid.

Step 16c: Shield as much of your assets as you legally can!

Why leave this up to the discretion of an FAO if your family gets aid based on your listed assets? Play it safe and shield those assets that you do not need to live on or need to use. But be careful to shield the assets in non-assessed assets or you will not be doing yourself any good. Colleges and universities began using enrollment management tactics and negotiation with students to attract the best students to meet the college's goals and increase revenue. A lot of these same colleges and universities have endowments in the billions and you should use every legal strategy to try to get some of that money to help with college costs.

Step 16d: Shield your assets in either an MEC or annuity.

Shield your assets as soon as you can and try to have them shielded by December 31st of the junior year of high school (no later than the date you file the financial aid forms). By moving your assets before the base year, the family will sidestep any assessment of the assets.

You can legally reposition assets to life insurance, pension funds, annuities, non-education IRAs, Keogh plans, Roth IRAs, and other retirement plans. As of today, I only recommend using either the life insurance (MECs) or annuities. With the right type of annuity or life insurance plan, you can guarantee the shielded assets will be safe, increase in value, be liquid, and most importantly be outside the financial aid formula radar! If your college money is invested in any type of financial product without security, it should be considered a "house of cards" waiting for a strong wind to blow it down.

Why do you need your money to be safe? If you are taking out student loans in your child's name and you are planning on using these assets to help you pay off this loan, you cannot risk that this money will lose value during the college years. Your money has to be invested into a financial product that has guarantees of principle.

Why do you need your money to be liquid? In case of an emergency, you might need this money. What if in two years you need $7,000 to pay for a new roof? You do not want to invest this money into a financial vehicle that will cost you a lot of money to withdraw the funds. You do not want to invest in any annuity or life insurance investment that has large withdrawal charges associated with it. Look for policies that have no withdrawal charge or cost $50 or less to get your money.

You have to do your homework on the insurance company. Not all insurance companies are safe, just like not all banks are safe. Since the start of the financial crisis in 2007, there have been 276 bank failures with assets totaling a staggering $627.2 billion.

First, you should check the company's "financial strength" ratings with ratings companies like Standard & Poor's, A.M. Best, and Moody's. Also, look at how long the company has been in business and the size of the company. I would suggest you not consider any company that has not been in business less than 50 years. To find out more ways to help you review insurance companies, go to my Web site at www.collegeaidfor middleclass.com.

In real estate investing, they tell you to "make your money on the purchase price, not on the sell price." If the value of the property happens to drop temporarily, you are still okay because you are not counting on a high sale price of the property to make you money. Much like real estate, when repositioning assets to an MEC or annuity, a family should make their return on the yearly college savings and not the return of the product.

While having a nice return is something to consider when evaluating different MECs and annuities, it should be the last factor. More important is the safety of your money while in the product, how liquid it is, and the financial strength of the company. If you do this the right way, you will get much more return from repositioning the assets when you save thousands, if not hundreds of thousands, of dollars in college savings!

A tax-deferred annuity is very similar to a CD. A CD is an agreement between a bank and an investor, while an annuity is an agreement between a life insurance company and an investor. While the CDs are taxed every year, the earnings in an annuity accumulate tax free until it is withdrawn. Usually the student is the beneficiary, while the annuitant can be the parent or the student. I do not recommend using a variable annuity because of the potential for loss of capital. I only recommend fixed or index annuities because of the guarantees not to lose principal. I would also only look for annuities that have a minimum penalty free withdrawal feature of 10% of accumulated value every year after the first year.

After the student graduates from college and the parents withdraw the money to pay off the loans, the insurance company will mail the family a 1099 with the total withdrawals and any taxable portion. The interest will be taxed as ordinary income and there is a 10% penalty tax *only on the gain* (*exceeds premiums paid*) if you take the withdrawal before age 59 ½. Would you rather pay a 10% penalty or have the college assess the assets assessed at a rate of 20% or higher *per year?*

I recommend using modified endowment contracts (MEC) life insurance products because they have the highest percentage of cash value compared to the death benefit. While having a death benefit is an added bonus, the primary reason a parent would invest in a life insurance policy is to shield the assets, protect the premiums from losses, and have the ability to get to the money easily and without high fees. Because the death benefit is easily the least important benefit, MECs work well to reduce insurance costs and expenses and maintain high cash surrender value. The death benefit amount will vary depending on amount of the premium and the insurer's age, sex, and health.

Much like the tax-deferred annuity, a withdrawal from an MEC (hopefully after college graduation) will usually cause a taxable event. Money invested into an MEC will be tax-deferred. If you withdraw the money before age 59 ½, you will pay regular income tax on the amount of policy gain and a 10% penalty on the gain. The policy gain is the difference between the cash value and the net investment in the policy.

If you design the MECs the correct way, you will benefit from:

1. No assessment of the assets from the colleges
2. Protection from the asset decreasing in value while the child is in college
3. Ability to access owner's money at all times without large fees
4. Death claim not subject to taxation

CHAPTER 30

STEP 17: Complete the Financial Aid Forms and Review the SAR Report

Regardless of the family's financial income, you must apply for financial aid using the appropriate financial aid forms. Most colleges and universities require the completion of financial aid forms to qualify for merit grants, scholarships, and student loans (Unsubsidized Stafford and PLUS). Be sure to check with each school on what forms need to be completed and when the deadlines are.

I remind my parents that this money is first come, first served. The FAFSA form should be completed during the first few weeks in January. Because the FAFSA will ask questions based upon the past year's income, most parents will wait until their taxes are complete to submit the form. Do not wait to have your taxes complete to fill out the FAFSA. Send in the form using estimated numbers based on your year-end statements and last year's tax return. Make sure you indicate on the FAFSA that you will be using only estimated numbers. Once your taxes are complete, update the FAFSA to reflect the numbers on your current tax return. Be sure to complete your taxes as soon as you can or ask your CPA to put you on the top of their list for completion.

The CSS Profile form due dates vary with the colleges. Some colleges require the CSS Profile form as early as November of the senior year.

The Student Aid Report (SAR) will be e-mailed or mailed to a family once the FAFSA has been submitted. On the SAR, you will see the family's calculated EFC. You should review this report to make sure the EFC you calculated earlier is close to the EFC indicated on the SAR report. If not, review your FAFSA for mistakes and/or contact the colleges to determine why.

CHAPTER 31

STEP 18: LEVERAGE: Suspend Admittance Decision Until You Evaluate All Financial Aid Award Letters

W hy should the child only pick colleges in which he or she is in the top 25% of the incoming freshmen? If you do this, you will know that it will be a good fit academically, the student will have enough free time to perform well academically, and the student will have enough downtime to enjoy himself or herself socially in college. Also, the student will be in a position to be offered wonderful co-ops and internships. **Most importantly, the colleges will see the child as someone they would like to recruit, and you will now have LEVERAGE.**

Most all colleges want to increase the number of students with high grades and SAT scores. **Because the student is someone they would like to recruit, the college is more willing to offer merit aid money or tuition discounts to encourage the student to attend their school!**

Leverage is the ability to do more with less. A lesson in the use of leverage needs to start out with an example to see how this works. If you had $10,000 to invest, you could purchase $10,000 in stock with a rate of return of 5% or use the $10,000 as a down payment to purchase $100,000 in real estate that also has a rate of return of 5%. While the initial purchase of $10,000 is the same, the $100,000 real estate purchase will generate more return through the use of leverage. The benefit of leverage is that you are able to use other people's money. In this case, it is the bank's money, which will accelerate the return on the investment.

Let's see an example of how a family can use leverage in college planning. A female student with a 1120 SAT score (not including the writing section), a 3.8 unweighted GPA, and who is in the top 10% of her class wants to attend a college to study journalism. The student applies to six colleges.

No Leverage: The student decided to attend a popular local in-state college that had good name recognition even though the campus was a little too large for the student's liking. She felt somewhat overwhelmed by the number of students on her college visit. The family knew her friends would be envious if she attended this particular college because the college was so prestigious. The college gladly accepted her because she was an average student compared to the other students on campus when they looked at her "college numbers." As a result, the college did not want to recruit the student because she was average in every way compared to most of the other freshman students that applied to the school. Moreover, the college believed it was not necessary to give out money to recruit good students because of its national name recognition. This college knew it could attract this family to the college to pay the full cost of tuition without sacrificing any of their multimillion dollar endowment. As a result, the college offered her no financial aid. While the family was happy that she was going to college, they knew that paying for the full cost of college of over $20,000 a year would be difficult.

Leverage: The student applied to 10 different colleges she would enjoy attending and was accepted at 8 out of the 10 schools. One of these colleges was of particular interest to her. It was a smaller, private college that had a wonderful reputation in journalism, and she felt very comfortable with the college when she visited. From their research, the family knew that the college did recruit freshmen by giving out non-need-based institutional aid as well as need-based aid. They also found out that her SAT score was in the top 75th percentile of the average freshmen at the school. Even though her friends did not recognize the name of the college, she fell in love with the campus and small class sizes. The college gladly accepted her and offered her admission to their honors program. The $42,000 cost of attendance at the college was drastically reduced by offering her college aid. The college wanted to recruit her, so they offered her grants and tuition discounts totaling $33,600 a year. This resulted in a final cost to the family of $8,400 a year.

Let's compare the long-term results of using leverage versus not using leverage. If the family decided on the non-leverage college choice, college would cost them $20,000 a year. Let's assume that the student will graduate in four years. That is a total cost of $80,000.

If the student attended the leveraged college, the result would be $8,400 a year for four years. This is a total cost of $33,600. That is an astonishing savings of $46,400 over four years for the same degree in journalism. Moreover, if she attended the leveraged college, she would have been in the honors program, where she would have been given special perks like registering for classes before other students and living in special dorms. I am sure the student would have considered this time the best four years of her life.

Conversely, if she attended the non-leveraged college, she would have been an average student at the college and blended in with every other student. In addition, because this is a large school with many students, being able to sign up for the classes that she needs to complete her major is very difficult and will probably extend her time at the college to at least five years. Now let's compare the total cost!

> In-state non-leveraged college:
> $20,000 x 5 years = $100,000
> VS
> Private leveraged college:
> $8,400 x 4 years = $46,400

Now the difference is **$53,600** and will continue to increase the longer the student stays in college.

The benefit of leverage is to use other people's money (in this case, the college's money) to maximize the return on investment. Not only will the cost of college be reduced and the student will probably enjoy her college experience more, but the student will be treated like an MVP by the college with the perks she receives in the honors program! The family did not allow others' opinions to influence their college choice, and they correctly found a college that was a perfect fit for the child. Because of their fact gathering, they also knew she had a great chance of the college offering her financial assistance.

Try to remain neutral and not become emotionally attached toward the colleges until you get the financial aid award letters from each school. By being neutral and not emotionally attached, you can make a better educated decision. Remember, every college has strengths and weaknesses.

How do you know if a college will want your student? Many parents think that just because their child is receiving numerous pieces of mail from ABC University that the school is interested in the student. This may or may not be true. I encourage parents to look at this activity as marketing rather than an expression of interest from the school. The ultimate expression of interest and the "final report card" is receiving a generous financial aid award letter from the college or university. Unfortunately, parents don't receive the financial aid award letters until late spring of the student's senior year.

If you take a top-down approach and narrow down your list from 6,500 colleges down to 6 to 10 schools (making sure they are schools that your child wants to attend), then you know which colleges use their money to recruit good students. And if the student is in the top 25% of the incoming freshman class, the family will be extremely happy with the results!

Please remember, being accepted at a college does not mean they want your child to attend. The colleges do "admit-deny" students in which they are given acceptance into the college, but the college offers no financial aid to the family knowing that they will probably not enroll because of the high price for the family. The only way to know if a college wants your child is to review the financial aid award letters. Do not tell any of the colleges where a student will be attending school until you have received all the financial aid award letters. You have until May 1st of the senior year to let the colleges know what your final selection is.

If you have followed my advice of applying to 6 to 10 colleges in which the student is in the top 25%, you should have many great financial aid award letters to review and compare.

Remember our second goal: fit and affordability. If the college is not affordable, it should not make the final cut.

For each award letter you receive, determine what, if any, your financial need is and how much need the college will meet. (COA − EFC = Financial Need). Did the college meet all the need or just some of the need? In

step 9, you found the **average merit aid and percentage of need met** by all the colleges on your list. Now you can compare your award letter to the average numbers you found earlier for that particular college to get a better idea of if the award letter is great, fair, or not good.

Case study: The Thomas family received a financial aid award letter from Elon University. The family's EFC was $20,035 and the COA for Elon University this year was $33,725. The financial need was calculated to be $13,690 ($33,725 - $20,035).

On the official financial aid award letter, the school offered the following financial aid:

Grants/scholarships:	$9,600
Loans/work-study:	$8,000

So the total financial aid was $17,600.

The parents knew when collecting facts about Elon University that the school only met 68% of the financial need on average. The family's need met was $13,690 based on the calculation of COA − EFC = FN, but they received $17,600 from the college. The college gave the family 129% of their need!

Moreover, from **step 9,** the family also knew that Elon University on average gives out $4,370 of merit aid per student. The family received $9,600 in merit aid from Elon! Can you tell if the college wanted this student or not? Obviously this was a great award letter from Elon College, and the family would be crazy to ask for more money from the college.

If you determine that the college only offered you average or below average merit aid or below the percentage of need met based upon historical data you gathered in **step 9,** you should appeal the letter. In some cases, I have seen appeals go as long as six months. (Go to my Web site at www.collegeaidformiddleclass.com for sample appeal letters.)

For example, from your *fact gathering data* from **step 9,** you already know that this particular college usually meets 100% of need and gives an average of $10,000 in aid per student. If the college only meets 50% of the need and only offers $3,000, then we know this is a poor financial aid award letter that should be appealed.

In the earlier case study, Elon offered the Thomas family an excellent award letter. However, the family would still need to come up with an additional $16,125 to cover the cost of college at Elon. This number is the amount of money parents will be borrowing in the student's name and will be saving in an MEC or annuity to pay off upon graduation.

The Thomas family also received award letters from Wake Forest University, University of North Carolina, and NC State. The Wake Forest University award letter offered the student the following:

The family's EFC was $20,035 and the COA for Wake Forest University that year was $49,032. The financial need was calculated to be $28,997 ($49,032 - $20,035).

On the official financial aid award letter, the school offered the financial aid as follows:

Grants/scholarships: $21,300
Loans/work-study: $9,500
So the need met was $30,800.

Wake Forest University on average gives out $11,071 of merit aid per student. The family received $21,300 in merit aid from Wake! Based upon the federal formula of COA – EFC = FN, the family's need was $28,997, but the college offered them $30,800 in aid. In essence, the family received $1,803 more than their calculated need. The family received another great award letter.

The next step is to compare this net cost to all the colleges to see what the bottom line cost will be at each college. The net cost of Wake Forest would be as follows:

Cost of Attendance: $49,032
Need Meet: $30,800 (total aid)
_____
Net cost to attend Wake: $18,232

The net cost to attend Elon University was $16,125.

Since UNC and NC State did not offer the family any scholarship or grants, the net cost at these two colleges for a North Carolina resident was $16,028 at NC State and $16,500 per year at UNC. The family now could choose between Elon at $16,125 per year, Wake at $18,232 per year, $16,028 at NC State, and $16,500 per year at UNC.

The student can now attend a private school for the same amount of money as an in-state public school. By following these steps, the cost of the college at each school is about equal in cost per year. It is up to the student and the family to decide which college is the best fit!

If a college is not affordable, take it out of consideration. At what price does the cost of college no longer make financial sense? **Remember, use your calculator, not your heart! Make sure you suspend all admittance decisions until you receive all the award letters and run the numbers.**

Finally, decide on a college that is the best fit for the student at the best price (fit and affordability, or, as I like to say, heart and calculator)! This way you will be paying *wholesale and not retail* college costs!

Education is a life-long process. Graduation from college is not the end; it's only the beginning.

When do you measure the success of a student's education? Some would argue it is measured by the final report card on the day of graduation from the college or university. I would think a better measure of success or effectiveness is when the student reaches retirement age and is able to look back on his or her life to see what he or she accomplished.

PARTING THOUGHTS

I have given you the 11 mistakes most families make that cost them thousands of dollars in college aid; I taught you the controversial principles and the behind-closed-door decision making of enrollment management and how the colleges use data mining and sophisticated computer models to help shape the compositions of the incoming freshmen class. I have also shown you the 19 steps to take that, applied effectively, you can use leverage to reduce the cost of college. I have not held anything back so you pay wholesale and not retail college cost! I am cheering for you to make college an affordable reality.

When I started this book, I had a goal of helping as many people afford the cost of college as possible. In order for me to achieve my goal, I need your help! With your assistance, we can make a huge impact in a life, we can make the dream of affording college come true, and we can change a small piece of the world by taking this 800-pound gorilla of paying for college off the backs of families. To make this happen, I need you to encourage other families to read, discuss, and apply the insights of this book.

Would you like to know how a family of four that had income of over $265,000, with over $342,000 in taxable investments, $150,000 in home equity, and an EFC of $99,999 was able to attend an out-of-state public college for only $12,590 a year? Please visit my Web site (www.collegeaid formiddleclass.com), and I will share with you their story and other real-life case studies of middle-income Americans just like you that successfully applied the principles that were discussed in this book. The book and these case studies validate and prove that what I teach and coach is true.

I would like to stay in touch and help you reach your goal of making college affordable. I eagerly look forward to meeting you and hearing about your success!

Ryan Clark, MBA, CCPS

STEP 19: The Forgotten Step: Working with a Coach or Advisor

"A single conversation across the table with a wise man
is worth a month's study of books."
– Chinese Proverb

One day I decided I should replace my hot water heater. It had been leaking water, and it had passed the average age of a hot water heater. I am fairly handy, and I am okay with tools. The hot water heater was located in my garage, and it was easy to get to. It was attached to my two small PVC pipes on the top. From my merchant seaman days, I worked a lot with plumbing and PVC piping, so I thought it would be pretty easy for me to do this job on my own and I would save a little money at the same time. One Saturday morning, I drove to the local store, and the salesman quoted me around $200 for a new water heater. I then added up the rest of the material I would need to complete the job, and it was going to cost me around $300 when all was said and done. While I was in the store looking at the water heater and getting ready to pay for my purchases, a neighbor recognized me and asked what I was doing. After I told him about my weekend job of replacing this hot water heater, he told me not to be stupid and hire his brother, a local plumber, to do the work for me. He said, "He can purchase this exact same water heater for $125, and he can install it for another $150." I immediately called his brother, and he installed the exact water heater for $25 less than if I had done it myself. Not only did I save money, but I saved my entire weekend. I learned that sometimes it's better to hire a professional!

This was a good lesson for me in working with a team of professionals. Life in general is a team sport, and no one should go at it alone! By following these steps, you will find predictable results and ultimate success.

No one climbs Mount Everest alone or dives to the bottom of the ocean alone. You should not try to climb this college planning mountain without the aid of others. The biggest risk we all face is not moving forward with what we learned. With a proper coach or an advisor, you can be taught the proper way to play this game and to make sure you move forward.

In my business, I coach families on how to achieve a college degree for less than they thought was possible by providing them with very simple, easy-to-follow steps. I have found that it is far superior to take one step at a time and complete that step than to try to complete multiple tasks all at the same time or to try to combine steps. Doing things without help will not save you time or energy.

With the help of Clark College Funding and our team, we will help a family keep the momentum needed to progress through these steps. It takes a lot of energy to get started with any new endeavor, but it takes far less energy to keep doing it once you get started. The simple rhythm of having a coach push you to complete these steps correctly soon becomes a part of a family's routine.

There is a lot of truth to the adage "you get what you pay for." Free advice is usually worth exactly what you paid for it: nothing! This especially holds true with college and college advisors. But when working with a coach or advisor who is trained in college financial planning and the nuances of financial aid, you will receive the "proper" advice.

This field is much more complex than most would have you believe. College has become too costly to navigate efficiently without help and without proper advice. Albert Einstein said, "Sometimes one pays most for the things one gets for nothing."

A good financial aid consultant will do more than complete the financial aid forms for you. A good coach or advisor will help you increase aid eligibility and also help with the college selection process, help narrow down the college choices for the student, and help the child narrow down what a student might want to study in college. A good college advisor will keep up to date with the specific state rules that govern aid. A good college advisor will also keep abreast of the ever-changing tax laws and regulations that will affect financial aid. A good advisor will know the "ins and outs" of enrollment management in order to maximize your chances to pay wholesale costs for college by maximizing a family's aid eligibility.

A good coach or mentor has the experience, attributes, and expertise in college planning. At Clark College Funding, Inc., we might not have the exact set of attributes and experience that you might want, but we do serve as a mentor, a motivator, a cheerleader, and a successful agent of accountability.

Change is the only thing that is constant in the world of financial aid and college funding. This past year, we have seen the FAFSA form change, the CSS Profile form change, educational tax credits change, and the federal student loan system change. It is a pretty safe assumption that it will continue to change every year and that the college costs will continue to rise! Based on recent history, it is never too early to start planning. If you have a *high school student*, this is the time to start planning to put strategies in place to take control of the cost of college and to begin implementing strategies to reduce this burden. With the help of Clark College Funding, Inc., we can make your dream of an affordable college education a reality.

It is time to for families to be in control of the college admissions and financial aid processes. It is time to bring back the dream of an affordable college education. It is time to reduce the stress of the student and his or her family during the student's senior year of high school. It is time to open up the world of possibilities and not to be limited by the cost of college. It is time to take the cost of college off the table when deciding on the best college fit for a child. It is time for someone to guide you and hold your hand to make sure you have a plan to pay for all your children!

Clark College Funding, Inc. has helped close to a thousand families with this burden, and we can do the same for you. We have been able to save on average $40,000 to $60,000 per child. It begins with our invitation to the *free* Web site. Simply go to www.collegeaidformiddleclass.com and follow the instructions provided! Let's get started!

> *"Life is a team sport, so choose your team carefully."*
> – Robert T. Kiyosaki

A Letter You Need to Read

February 12, 2008

To Whom It May Concern:

I am happy to furnish this letter of recommendation for Ryan Clark and his team. I have used the services they offer and experienced what they can do for both students and parents. I have also given telephone references for them both and assured people that the cost of this program is returned many times over. Most people who have called me have been interested in how the "numbers" work. They sometimes do not understand the business side of this transaction and how the parties are compensated. In going through the process, the advantages offered will become obvious. I am a fan of Ryan and have found him to be straightforward, trustworthy, and always willing to help. Ryan and his staff have also been invaluable to us. Everything we went through was necessary and helpful.

The career counseling they offered verified the engineering plans my son had in mind. The school selection process, however, completely turned us around. We were set on one of three large public institutions and had no plans to apply to private schools. He insisted that we not only apply, but visit.

My son's final selection was a school that we had barely heard of and did not know that they even offered engineering as a major. When we visited, we were amazed. They not only had the best facilities of any school we visited, but they had the best program, far and away.

The cost was $38,400 per year. **Our "out of pocket" for the first semester was $113!**

Because my son's savings are "protected," he will graduate with the ability to pay all of his student loans and have money left over. This would not be possible without Ryan's help... He got us through the entire FAFSA and application process for eight schools.

We had "inside information" about all the schools and with CCF's help were able to negotiate an excellent package. We simply would not have chosen the school we picked or made it through all the paperwork without CCF's help.

My son finished his first semester with a 3.75 GPA, on the dean's list, and as a member of the Psi Eta Sigma National Honors Fraternity. He loves the school and his life on campus. We simply cannot imagine that we could be in a better situation or be happier.

Ed Machen

Edmund Hammond Machen

BONUS CHAPTERS

As much as I wanted to share with you all the secrets and strategies that can help with the college game, I could not because of space constraints. Use passwords hidden in this book to access some of the best advice I have to offer. Listed below is just a sample of the information you can collect:

Tax Planning for College

What's the best form for new business?

10 Ways to Make College an Affordable Reality

For this reader-only content, please visit my companion Web site and free how-to blog at www.collegeaidformiddleclass.com!

COLLEGE TERMINOLOGY YOU MAY NEVER HEAR

ADMIT-DENY: Process of ranking students who have already been accepted to the college. I.e., a college wants 500 freshmen, so it mails 1,200 acceptance letters and uses aid to entice the 300 most-wanted students.

APPLICATION SCORE: A scoring system used (in different formats) by every college. It is how they rank their applicants. Some colleges use a number system or letter system to sort. Most colleges will have an applicant's package read by two admissions officers. If your student's score is above the cutoff mark, they are admitted. If the score is below the mark, they are rejected. If the score is in between the marks, a committee determines the student's fate.

BUYING FRESHMEN: The students who are most attractive to a college get the best financial aid package with more grants and free money and fewer loans and less work-study. This can also be in the form of large tuition discounts or giving more aid than the calculated financial need.

FLAG: A student's record has been marked for special consideration (i.e., children of alumni, students with special talents, or underrepresented minorities). These applications usually are separated from the common pool and considered separately.

FINANCIAL AID LEVERAGING: The practice of cutting the cost of attendance for specifically targeted groups of applicants. The goal is to maximize the financial aid dollar and admit larger numbers of students with the same dollars. The school may also artificially depress the amount of aid given in a year to see if that level of aid can become the new "baseline."

GENDER BALANCE: Some colleges have specific requirements for ratios of men to women in the student body. The admissions and financial aid offices then attempt to build a class with these predetermined characteristics.

LEGACY RATING: Children of alumni are called legacies, and sometimes these students have an advantage over others during the admissions process but not the financial aid process. The size of this advantage may be determined by the generosity in alumni fund drives.

PREFERENTIAL PACKAGING: This is the politically correct term for buying freshmen. Fifty-four percent of colleges "admit" to following this practice.

HELPFUL DEFINITIONS

Cost of attendance: This number will differ at each school. It includes tuition, fees, room and board, books and materials, transportation costs, and living expenses.

Dependent students: Students who are dependent on their parents for support. Both the parents' and the student's income and assets are evaluated when determining how much a family can contribute towards college costs.

Expected family contribution: The amount a student and his or her family are judged capable of paying. The contribution remains constant no matter where the student plans to attend college.

Full-time student: Students must take a minimum of 12 credit hours per term to be considered a full-time student.

Grants and scholarships: They are both considered gift aid since they do not have to be repaid. They are the most desirable forms of financial aid.

Independent students: Students who are not dependent on their parents for support. Only the student's income and assets and those of a spouse are evaluated when determining a contribution towards college costs. Generally, students must be at least 24 years of age by December 31 of the award year to qualify as an independent. Students with legal dependents also qualify. Married and graduate students also qualify as independent students.

Loans: These are sums of money that must be repaid. The reason they count as financial aid is that they contain favorable repayment terms and are offered at attractive interest rates below the going commercial rate.

Merit-based aid: Merit-based financial aid programs determine eligibility by evaluating a student's ability and potential based on academic records or athletic or artistic ability. Individual characteristics, such as ethnicity, are sometimes considered.

Need-based aid: Need-based financial aid programs determine eligibility by evaluating the family's resources.

Part-time student: To qualify for most federal student aid programs, a student must take six credit hours per term.

Student aid application: Every student who wants to apply for any of the federal student aid programs, some of the campus-based student aid programs, and some of the state student aid programs must first complete the federally approved student aid application. This is called the Free Application for Federal Student Aid (FAFSA). Students may also be required to fill out additional forms such as the Financial Aid Profile (FAP) for a small fee if the college to which they are applying or the state in which they live requires additional information for awarding their own funds.

Work-study: This is exactly what it sounds like. It is money that does not have to be repaid, and the college will provide the student with the job. Work-study jobs pay minimum wage. The work commitment is fulfilled once the student has earned the amount of work-study awarded.

Resource Guide

Academic Accreditation Agencies

Council for Higher Education Accreditation:
www.chea.org/directories/special.asp

U.S. Department of Education's Database of Accredited Postsecondary Institutions and Programs: http://ope.ed.gov/accreditation

Academic Quality

College Navigator, Institute of Education Sciences, National Center for Education Statistics: www.nces.ed.gov/collegenavigator

Community College Survey of Student Engagement: www.ccsse.org

The Education Conservancy: www.educationconservancy.org

National Survey of Student Engagement: www.nsse.iub.edu

Center of Inquiry in the Liberal Arts at Wabash College:
www.liberalarts.wabash.edu

The Teagle Foundation: www.teaglefoundation.org

Canadian Schools

Association of Universities and Colleges of Canada: www.aucc.ca

SchoolFinder.com: www.schoolfinder.com

My Career Profile:
www.careerdimension.com/register/collegefundingservicecenter.cfm

Discover by ACT: https://actapps.act.org/eDISCOVER

CLEP Guides

CLEP Practice Exams: www.collegeboard.com/clep

CLEP Test Study Guides: www.finishcollegefast.com/clep

Pass the CLEP Test: www.acetheclep.com

College Advisors

National Institute of Certified College Planners: www.niccp.com

National College Advocacy Group: www.ncagonline.org
Higher Education Consultants Association: www.hecaonline.org

Independent Educational Consultants Association:
    www.educationalconsulting.org

College Applications

Common Application: www.commonapp.org

Colleges for Athletes

Future Athletes: www.futureathletes.com

Ivy League Sports: www.ivyleaguesports.com

National Association of Collegiate Directors of Athletics: www.nacda.com

National Collegiate Athletic Association: www.ncaa.org

National Scouting Report: www.nsr-inc.com

Colleges for the Learning Disabled and Those with Special Needs

Americans with Disabilities Act: www.ada.gov/

Attention Deficit Disorder Association: www.add.org

Children and Adults with Attention Deficit/Hyperactivity Disorder: www.chadd.org

Council for Exceptional Children: www.cec.sped.org

Hoagies' Gifted Education Page: www.hoagiesgifted.com

LD Online: www.ldonline.org

Learning Disabilities Association of America: www.ldanatl.org

National Center for Learning Disabilities: www.ncld.org

Smart Kids with Learning Disabilities: www.smartkidswithld.org

Colleges for International Students and Study Abroad

American Institute for Foreign Study: www.aifs.org

Canada School Finder: www.schoolfinder.com

Council on International Educational Exchange: www.ciee.org

eduPass: www.edupass.org

Institute for International Education: www.iie.org

NAFSA: Association of International Educators: www.nafsa.org

U.S. Government Visa Information: http://travel.state.gov/visa/

UK Universities and College Application Services: www.ucas.ac.uk

College Selection Guides

College Search Engines

1) College View:
   www.collegeview.com/collegesearch/advSearch.jsp?partner=
   &newSearch=true
2) Collage Board:
   http://collegesearch.collegeboard.com/search/index.jsp

3) Princeton Review:
   www.princetonreview.com/com.aspx?uidbadge=%07
4) Carnegie Foundation:
   http://classifications.carnegiefoundation.org/lookup_listings/
   institution.php?key=782
5) Federal College Navigator: www.nces.ed.gov/collegenavigator

College Additional Research Information

1) College Confidential: www.collegeconfidential.com

2) College Results: www.collegeresults.org

3) Virtual Tours: www.campustours.com

4) University TV Tours: www.youniversitytv.com

5) Elite College Debt Consideration Table:
   http://projectonstudentdebt.org/files/pub/Yale_pledge_RS_
   FINAL.pdf

6) Christian College Assistance Site:
   www.christiancollegementor.org

7) Jewish College Assistance Site: www.hillel.org

Community Colleges

Community College Survey of Student Engagement: www.ccsse.org

Jack Kent Cooke Foundation: www.jackkentcookefoundation.org

Phi Theta Kappa: www.ptk.org

Financial Aid

Clark College Funding: www.clarkcollegefunding.com

Economic Diversity of Colleges: www.economicdiversity.org

Federal Student Aid Guide: http://studentaid.ed.gov

FedMoney.org: www.fedmoney.org

FinAid: www.finaid.org

FinancialAidLetter.com: www.financialaidletter.com

National Association of Student Financial Aid Administrators:
www.nasfaa.org

Nelnet Education Planning and Financing: www.nelnet.com

Paying for College with the Greenes on PBS:
www.pbs.org/payingforcollege

U.S. Department of Education, Federal Student Aid:
www.studentaid.ed.gov

Financial Aid Applications

CSS/Financial Aid Profile: http://profileonline.collegeboard.com

Free Application for Federal Student Aid (FAFSA): www.fafsa.ed.gov

529 Plans

Independent 529 Plan: www.independent529plan.org

Morningstar: www.morningstar.com

SavingForCollege.com: www.savingforcollege.com

General College Application Resources

ACT: www.act.org

All About College: www.allaboutcollege.com

Campus Outreach Services: www.campusoutreachservices.com

Campus Tours Online: www.campustours.com

Cattlemen's Texas Longhorn Conservancy: www.ctlc.org

Chronicle of Higher Education: www.chronicle.com

College Board: www.collegeboard.com

College Board: Issues and Trends: www.collegeboundnews.com

College Prowler: www.collegeprowler.com

College View: www.collegeview.com

College Week Live: www.collegeweeklive.com

Collegiate Choice Walking Tours: www.collegiatechoice.com

Collegiate Way Residential Colleges: www.collegiateway.org

Education Conservancy: www.educationconservancy.org

Education Trust: www.collegeresults.org

Education Week: www.edweek.org

Educational Testing Service: www.ets.org

Greene's Guides: www.greenesguides.com

Institute for Higher Education Policy Rankings Clearinghouse:
    www.ihep.org

Kaarme: www.kaarme.com

Kaplan: www.kaplan.com

National Association for College Admission Counseling:
    www.nacacnet.org

National Center for Education Statistics:
    www.nces.ed.gov/collegenavigator

National Center for Fair and Open Testing: www.fairtest.org

National Survey of Student Engagement: www.nsse.iub.edu

Number2 Free Test Prep: www.number2.com

Peterson's: www.petersons.com

Princeton Review: www.review.com

Ten Steps to College with Greenes on PBC:
   www.pbs.org/tenstepstocollege

U.S. News & World Report: www.usnews.com/sections/education

U101 College Search: www.u101.com

Unigo: www.unigo.com

YOUniversity Online Tours: www.youniversity.tv

Graduation Rates

College Navigator, Institute of Education Sciences, National Center for
   Education Statistics: www.nces.ed.gov/collegenavigator

The Education Trust's College Results Online: www.collegeresults.org

Higher Education Press Coverage and Trends

The Chronicle of Higher Education: www.chronicle.com

Inside Higher Ed: www.insidehighered.com

The Journal of Blacks in Higher Education: www.jbhe.com

New America Foundation's Higher Ed Watch Blog:
   www.newamerica.net/blog/higher_ed_watch

College Board's Trends in Higher Education:
   http://professionals.collegeboard.com/data-reports-research/trends

Interviews

A Pocket Guide to Choosing a College: Are You Asking the Right Questions?:
   http://nsse.iub.edu/html/students_parents.cfm

Learning Communities

Residential Learning Communities International Clearinghouse, Bowling Green State University: http://pcc.bgsu.edu/rlcch

Washington Center for Improving the Quality of undergraduate Education: www.evergreen.edu/washcenter/project.asp?pid=73

Minorities and Colleges

A Better Chance: www.abetterchance.org

American Council on Education: www.acenet.edu

Association of Black Admissions and Financial Aid Officers of the Ivy League and Sister Schools: www.abaschools.org

AVID: www.avid.org

Black Collegian: www.black-collegian.com

Black Excel: www.blackexcel.org

Bureau of Indian Education: U.S. Department of the Interior: www.bie.edu

College Fund/UNCF: www.uncf.org

The Congressional Hispanic Caucus Institute: www.chci.org

Economic Diversity of Colleges: www.economicdiversity.org

The HBCU (Historically Black Colleges and Universities) Network: www.hbcunetwork.com

Hispanic Association of Colleges & Universities: www.hacu.net

Hispanic Scholarship Fund: www.hsf.net

Historically Black Colleges and Universities and National Association for Equal Opportunity: www.nafeo.org/community

The Journal of Blacks in Higher Education: www.jbhe.com

KnowHow2Go: www.knowhow2go.com

NAACP: www.naacp.org

National Association of Hispanic Publications Foundation's Scholarships for Hispanics: www.scholarshipsforhispanics.org

Pathways to College Network: www.pathwaystocollege.net

QuestBridge: www.questbridge.org

Tribal College Journal of American Indian Higher Education: www.tribalcollegejournal.org

Online Applications and Research

Common Application: www.commonapp.org

Embark: www.embark.com

Naviance: www.naviance.com

Universal College Application: www.universalcollegeapp.com

Xap: www.xap.com

Private Colleges and Universities

Common Data Set: To find each school's "Common Data Set," type the term into the institution's online search engine.

Council of Independent Colleges: www.cic.edu/makingthecase

The Education Trust's College Results Online: www.collegeresults.org

National Association of Independent Colleges and Universities: www.naicu.edu

University and College Accountability Network (U-CAN): www.ucan-network.org

SAT/ACT Guides and Preparation

ACT Test Dates 2010-2011: www.actstudent.org/regist/currentdates.html

ACT: www.act.org

ePrep: www.eprep.com

National Center for Fair and Open Testing (FairTest): www.fairtest.org

Number2.com: www.number2.com

SAT (College Board): http://sat.collegeboard.com/practice

SAT Subject Test Schools:
    www.compassprep.com/admissions_req_subjects.aspx

SAT Test Dates 2010-2011: http://sat.collegeboard.com/register/sat-dates

Scholarship Guides

Scholarship Search Engine Resources

1) Merit Aid: www.meritaid.com
2) Fastweb: www.fastweb.com
3) Sallie Mae: www.salliemae.com/before_college/students_plan/
   free_money/scholarship-search.htm
4) College Met: www.mach25.com

Local Scholarships Resource Links

1) Community Foundations: Search for Community
   Foundations + Scholarships

2) Scholarship America:
   http://scholarshipamerica.org/chapter_search.php

3) Guaranteed-Scholarships: www.guaranteed-scholarships.com

4) College Board's Scholarship Search:
   http://apps.collegeboard.com/cbsearch_ss/welcome.jsp

5) Federal Trade Commission:
   www.ftc.gov/scholarshipscam (877) FTC-HELP

6) Scholarships.com: www.scholarships.com

7) National Merit Scholarship Corporation:
   www.nationalmerit.org

8) SchoolGrantsBlog.com: www.schoolgrantsblog.com

Student Loans

Credit Bureaus:

Equifax: (800) 685-1111: www.equifax.com

Experian: (888) 397-3742: www.experian.com

TransUnion: (800) 888-4213: www.transunion.com

FinAid: www.finaid.com

National Consumer Law Center's Student Loan Borrower
   Assistance project: www.studentloanborrowerassistance.org

Project on Student Debt: www.projectonstudentdebt.org

StudentLoanJustice.org: www.studentloanjustice.org

Study Guides

Master Student Program:
   http://college.hmco.com/collegesurvival/ellis/master_student/10e/
   students/toc.html#ch01

Cornell Note Taking System: www.eleven21.com/notetaker

HippoCampus: www.hippocampus.org

Teacher Evaluations

MyEdu: www.myedu.com

ProfessorPerformance.com: www.professorperformance.com

RateMyProfessors.com: www.ratemyprofessors.com

Textbooks

Amazon.com: www.amazon.com

Barnes & Noble: www.barnesandnoble.com

Best Book Buys: www.bestbookbuys.com

Undergraduate Research

Council on Undergraduate Research: www.cur.org

Web Guide to Research for Undergraduates (WebGURU): www.webguru.neu.edu

Working Colleges

Working Colleges Consortium: www.workcolleges.org

Acknowledgements

I have not attempted to cite in the text all the authorities and sources consulted in the preparation of this manual. To do so would require more space than is available. The list would include departments of various governments, libraries, industrial institutions, periodicals, and many individuals.

I would like to begin by thanking Brian Ward, owner of the College Authority, and Mike Davila, a college financial expert in Texas who helped me begin my journey and taught me most of what I know today. Without their help and knowledge, this book could not have been written.

I am indebted to Rick Darvis, CPA, and Ron Them, who are the founder and cofounder of the National Institute of Certified College Planners. They opened my eyes to the wonderful "tax scholarships" available. I'm also grateful to Al Hoffman, cofounder of the National College Advocacy Group (NCAG) and president and founder of The College Funding Service Center, for his insight and for answering the many questions I had for him.

In addition, I would like to thank Mark Kantrowitz, the founder of FinAid.org, whose understanding and grasp of college financing was invaluable. Robert J. Massa, vice president for enrollment and college relations at Dickinson College, was helpful in his insight on college admissions. I would also like to thank Leslie Chase, college resource teacher at Pine View School, for her thoughts, as well as Manuel Fabriquer, CCPS, DDC, owner of College Planning ABC in California, and Cori Murphy, CCPS, owner of The College Authority in Oregon, for their wonderful peer review and analysis.

I am appreciative of Jeff Foley, CPA, president of Carolina Tax Advisory Group, for his opinions and his unique perspective of having a child who is a senior in high school. I would also like to express thanks to Mary Jane Freeman, M.A.Ed., president of The Davidson Center, for her vision and views on finding the right college for a student. A big thank you also goes to Renée Anthony Leak, director of High Schools and

ThinkCOLLEGE, and Mary Alice Katon, director of College Access Programs Communities In Schools.

I am also indebted to two of my clients that contributed greatly to this book, Ed Machen and Bonnie Wright. Working with wonderful families like the Wrights and Machens is what makes my job the best job in the world.

Of course, I would like to thank my wife, Rosie Clark, and our children, Caden and Carlene, who motivated me to write this book and who always gave their loving support. Finally, I have to thank my mother, Darlene Clark, for her help and assistance.

About the Author

Ryan Clark, MBA, CCPS is the president and principal educational strategist of Clark College Funding, Inc. Since 2003, he has gained extensive experience helping families throughout the Carolinas with their college planning. He holds designations from the National Association of College Financial Advisors, is a member of the National College Advocacy Group, and is a Certified College Planner.

Ryan uses unique and cutting-edge tax, financial, and academic strategies to provide families with affordable solutions for the high cost of education. Ryan also implements strategic cash flow planning to show families how to pay for college without changing their lifestyles or affecting their retirement plans.

He is often invited to speak at high schools, PTSA groups, libraries, and professional groups. Ryan holds an MBA from Queens University in Charlotte and is an alumnus of the United States Merchant Marine Academy, where he earned an ABET accredited bachelor's degree in marine systems engineering.

Ryan is a retired lieutenant in the U.S. Naval Reserve and held a U.S. Coast Guard License as a Third Assistant Engineer (unlimited tonnage).

Key Frustrations and Concerns:

❖ Isn't it surprising that **80% of all students** change their major once?

❖ Did you know on average, college students change their major **3 TIMES** over the course of their college career?

❖ Do you think *changing majors* can *increase the cost of college*?

❖ Did you know there are ***over 6,500*** colleges, universities, technical institutions, and vocational training institutes?

❖ Are you surprised that **both public and private schools are graduating just 37% of their full time students in 4 yrs.**?

❖ Can you believe that over **60% of students** in the U.S. who enroll in either a four-year or two-year College will **probably transfer**?

❖ Do you think attending the wrong school and *transferring* to another college will *increase the cost of college*?

❖ Are you surprised that some Colleges give about the **same weight to your SAT/ACT score as your ENTIRE GPA**?

❖ Do you think it is worth spending a few minutes each day to study for these tests?

❖ Do you think the FAFSA form is free? (Free Application for Federal Student Aid)

❖ Are you surprised to know that the Dept. of Education states that 80% of all the FAFSA forms are done incorrectly?

❖ Do you think if parents complete the forms wrong, it could cost them a lot of money in aid? (i.e. $3,000 in lost aid * 5 yrs. of college = $15,000 in lost aid)

❖ Do you still think the FAFSA form is free?

- ❖ Do you realize that students and parents are so befuddled by financial aid that they end up making expensive mistakes, such as taking out unnecessarily expensive loans?

- ❖ Can you believe schools continue to ask deep probing financial questions including; Home Equity, Retirement Accounts, Cars, 529 Plans, and much more!

- ❖ Do you now think the colleges can be more intrusive than the IRS about your personal finances?

- ❖ If the EFC number is the minimum amount of money the government says you can afford to pay for college, *wouldn't it be wise to know your family's EFC before the government tells you what it is?*

- ❖ If colleges know it is possible to legally and ethically reduce a family's EFC number, why don't they inform every parent on how to do it?

- ❖ **If Clark College Funding Inc. parents do not overpay for college, why should you?**

Yes, let's get started and take the first step!

For a limited time, I will *waive the regular $165.00 fee* and provide you with a **valuable 30 minute telephone consultation for FREE** with one of my key staff members to help you find *affordable solutions for the High Cost of Education.*™

Two Easy Ways to Contact Us:

1 Visit our website
   www.collegeaidformiddleclass.com
   or **www.clarkcollegefunding.com**

2 Call us at **704-944-3543**

TUITION PUBLISHING

Charlotte, NC

CPSIA information can be obtained
at www.ICGtesting.com
Printed in the USA
FFOW02n1636310116
20804FF